C000025571

A comedians guide to the city

Edited by Tim Clark and Andrew Mickel

With contributions from over 150 of the best acts in the comedy business

suchsmallportions.com

SECRET EDINBURGH

First published July 2013 by Such Small Portions.

Text copyright © 2013 Such Small Portions.

Printed by Mega Printing, www.mega.com.tr

NICA BURNS

// FOREWORD //

I've been going to the Edinburgh Festival every year since 1982 as a performer, director, producer and audience member. I've had a ball. If only I'd had this book from the very first day….

Edinburgh is in itself a fantastic city, transformed into a fabulous carnival during the Fringe. The collective experience of the writers of this quirky, off-beat guide to their Secret Edinburgh during the festival adds up to decades. This book will help you make the most of your time when you're not watching a show—from finding that quiet get-away-from-it-all moment by a babbling brook or a mound with a view — to where to enjoy the best vegetarian haggis or finest curry. Or where to go dancing, drink with the performers, not drink with the performers, or experience a magical sunrise.

This is without doubt the best, most original and—as it's written by comedians—extremely entertaining guide to enjoying every minute of your time at the Edinburgh Festival. Secret Edinburgh is a must-have and no serious Fringe-goer should be without it.

Nica Burns
Theatre producer
Director, Foster's Edinburgh Comedy Awards

INTRODUCTION

If we were to credit anyone with helping to inspire this book it would have to be Lucy Porter.

Tuning into a local Edinburgh radio station just before lunchtime during the Edinburgh Fringe in 2010, I was greeted by an interview with the comedian where she was asked what she was doing apart her shows. In her answer Lucy talked so enthusiastically about this amazing local baked potato shop that by the time she had finished I had stopped whatever I was doing and caught myself staring forlornly at a bare fridge, wondering, just where is this incredible little eatery?

Heading out to hunt down Lucy's recommendation, it struck me that of all the people who you could ask for tips on where to go in Edinburgh, comedians would have to rank among the best.

They are the most obsessive visitors a city could ever wish for. Each August thousands of acts pack their suitcase for a month-long migration to Scotland's capital to join the madness of the world's biggest arts festival.

Over the years they have had time to try every dish, find every late night bar, and head as far as possible away from the festival they happen to have made such effort to take part in.

Indeed, some comedians who we have interviewed for this book have spent over 20 consecutive summers at the festival. We tried to work out how many festivals had been attended by our 170 contributors and around 1,000 emerged as a low estimate. Condensed down, that's a lifetime of Edinburgh as a tourist.

And what contributors they are: from the big TV stars who know how to fill up for a fiver to newcomers who head to the classiest restaurants, together they've covered the city from the top of Arthur's Seat (Joel Dommett) to the bottom of Broughton Street (Colin Hoult).

The results have been outstanding. In these pages you'll find out who is giving restaurant tips to Hardeep Singh Kohli, why Jonny & The Baptists keep ending up in A&E, how Mark Thomas relaxes during the festival, and what Milton Jones is up to loitering in the corridors of the Pleasance.

Though this book isn't a traditional travel guide; our maps aren't particularly useful, some of the things written about are possibly dangerous, and our directions include 'howling at the moon', we do hope that it gives the reader a sense of what Edinburgh is about that can't be filtered down on a smart phone or found on a 'top ten' list.

Secret Edinburgh is in essence a love letter to the city masquerading as travel literature. However, if we wish one thing, it is that you have as much fun in this beautiful city as we and the performers who have contributed to this guide have had over years.

And don't forget to howl at the moon once in a while!

Tim Clark and Andrew Mickel

CONTENTS

© Guy Alastair

FRINGE SURVIVAL GUIDE

REMEMBER TO EAT HEALTHILY

During the Fringe, I find it helpful to treat your body like a venue. Sure, you've prepared it nicely, wiped it down, and sprayed it with disinfectant, but now you have to deal with the punters. Some punters, like apples and cereal, will treat your venue with respect, lining up patiently and quietly filing out when the show is over.

Other punters, unfortunately, have less regard for your interior performance space. I'm talking chips, beer, and Aberdeen Angus beef burgers.

These guys will normally rock up with a mate on a 2-for-1 pass, or even sneak inside when you are looking the other way. At the end of the show, they will be in no hurry to leave, and you can be sure when they do, it will be a loud and unpleasant experience. In short: drink water, eat vitamins. **Sammy J**

GET YOUR BEARINGS - OR GET OUT OF TOWN

Edinburgh is small for a European capital, and small considering its history and cultural importance. London, where I live, is a collection of villages. Edinburgh is a single village. Everybody knows everybody else's business.

Nevertheless, Edinburgh's bigger than you think. Some Fringegoers never leave the Pleasance Courtyard, lest they should meet someone Scottish. Many others dare to go as far as the Fringe Office, and the brave ones may even slither down The Mound (oh, the double-entendres available here) as far as Princes Street.

Many years ago, when my own show was at a Grassmarket venue, a couple told me: "we've been looking for you all Fringe, but we didn't realise you were so far from the centre."

But there's a lot more to Edinburgh than where the Fringe is. And a day ticket unlocks it. Last year I discovered the 26, along the coast of the Firth; beautiful in a way that comedy is not. And at the end of the line, the driver wanted me off. I told him I had a day ticket and was going back. He said: Ah'm no' goin' back.

Struck by omens, I thought: right. Then neither am I. It didn't last, of course. But I had thrown my fate to the wind of the random Lothian bus. Go thou and do thou likewise. On thy day off, of course. Who needs trams? **Peter Buckley Hill**

HOW TO FLYER LIKE A PRO

Here is my invaluable guide to the art of flyering to help you get through day in, day out, through earth, wind, fire (not much) and rain (lots). First up, some dos and don'ts.

- DON'T stand still, holding your flyers in a pretentious mime pose. Passers by may take your flyer but they won't see your show.
- DO simulate sex. Passers by may not take your flyer but they will see your show.
- DON'T run up to people and shout in their faces; you will be killed.
- DO sing, play musical instruments and have gorgeous girls in your cast. Crowds will gather and you may even inadvertently raise some cash from busking. It all helps.

Next, the nitty gritty: how to get through a long shift without going insane.

- Ideally you need to flyer with someone else. A flyering session you share is a flyering session you survive.
- Pretend crowds are made up of celebrities. It is great fun imagining you are really flyering Brad, Angelina or Clint.

Although in my time I have flyered Billy Connolly, Jeremy Paxman and H from Steps.

- Come up with some rhymes about your show that can keep your soul calm and be used as a mantra: "Don't buy an omelette, come and see Hamlet"; "My house is on fire, please take my flyer"; "Make your choose-ical to watch our musical".

Finally, how do you actually get people to take your flyer?

- Set up your pitch, ideally on the Royal Mile. This will be your home.
- Don't be a twat. People won't take one. Would you?
- People love free. Just shout "free thing" a lot and the public will come to you.
- Lie and say "sell-out show, five stars". If you get caught out on this, just say "bonjour" and run away. **Dan from The Real MacGuffins**

HOW TO AVOID GETTING A COLD

I used to get two colds a year. One came just after Christmas, when the happiness and hope of the season gets thrown out with the last of the turkey and January turns to drizzle.

The second started the moment I boarded the train to Edinburgh for the festival. By mid-morning the following day, the dry tickle in the back of my throat would be replaced by a sensation of swallowing freshly salted broken glass while sucking on a grapefruit, and my temperature would be as high as the hopes of the sixth form musical theatre troupe flyering in the dank.

Over the next two weeks, this cold would inevitably evolve into a disease of plague-like proportions, brought on by talking for an hour a day in a room that is essentially a petri dish with lights and a microphone. These 'venues' vapourise the bacteria of all in attendance, creating a thick layer of condensation and scum on all surfaces, and then drips it down on one particular spot. Usually the performer's head.

These days, things are a bit more refined. I flee the country in winter and get to perform at the King Dome, Pleasance, which even has air conditioning. But what if you do get sick? How to recover?

Here's my secret. Turbo Lemsip. Yes. Turbo. Lemsip. In layman's terms, it is Lemsip with some vitamins and a few extra ingredients. But that is a bit like saying the Great Wall of China is just made up of bricks, mortar and suffering. So let me break it down for you.

FInd some Max Strength Lemsip. If you are counting the pennies, Boots' own brand substitute will do. Drop in a Berocca. Hear that fizz? That's the sound of goodness dissolving. It's a metaphor. Next add some honey (preferably Manuka), fresh ginger, and if you are a drinker, whisky to the mix.

Have one of these bad boys every four hours and your cold will vanish quicker than the hopes of the aforementioned musical theatre troupe. Also, you will be drunk. Which is by far the best way to experience the festival. **Piff**

WHAT TO DO IN AN EMERGENCY

Royal Infirmary of Edinburgh, 51 Little France Crescent, EH16 4SA. 0131 536 1000, or just find a friendly local paramedic.

Paddy, who plays lead guitar in the Baptists, is, to put it mildly, fucking clumsy.

He's a good person. He's an exceptional musician. He washes regularly. He's kind to animals. His Dad is proud of him. But to say he is 'a bit injury-prone' is the most generous way to describe the world's most blundering, ham-handed, maladroit, stumbling idiot in comedy today.

We've been to hospital when he's fallen off from climbing a bookshelf to check something. We've been to hospital when he ate a whole cigarette (by mistake - I mean, it's unbelievable). He tried to stand on a basketball and broke his wrist. He tried to impress someone by doing a front flip off a chair and fell entirely into a bin. He once shot himself with a crossbow. He once hit himself in the leg with an axe. On two separate occasions he has 'got a rock stuck up his nose'. He is, essentially, anti-Darwinian.

So our favourite place in Edinburgh, without a shadow of a doubt, has got to be the Accident and Emergency Department of Edinburgh's Royal Infirmary. It's a regular Baptists haunt. After all, one of us is clinically hazardous.

Last year, Paddy slipped on an onstage puddle whilst we were performing on Marcus Brigstocke's Early Edition in the Udderbelly. He went down like a sack of limbs and smashed his guitar over his arm, but the adrenaline drove us on and we finished the gig. Six minutes later we walked offstage and a very worried Susan Calman helped us get Paddy into a cab and straight to the hospital. Jonny had to sit fidgeting in the waiting room where he spent all of his money on buying eleven packs of Skittles from the vending machine.

The doctors, the nurses and all the staff are just so lovely at The Edinburgh Royal Infirmary. It's a shame they don't offer accommodation there for the whole month, we'd save a fortune. Plus we already have the WiFi password. **Jonny and the Baptists**

HOW TO IMPRESS A DATE

Oh hello there. I'm Mark Restuccia. I'm probably one of the most prolific internet daters in my weight class. I've been on over 1,500 dates and have turned into somewhat of a serial dater over the years. But don't worry—I only date other serial daters these days. I'm like the Dexter of the dating world, if you will.

Now, it is too late for me to find my soul mate, due to crowing about my un-dateability at comedy festivals, in glossy magazines and the like, but it is not too late for me to offer a bit advice.

So you want to go on a date with somebody, eh? You sly old dog! Well first of all, here are a couple of types of places to try and aim for to make that crucial first date bearable.

- Find a quiet bar somewhere neutral, away from the places where you both work to lower the risk of being busted on a date by colleagues.

- You don't want a noisy bar either, or you run the risk of not being able to hear what your potential love interest has to say. This may or may not be a good thing.

- You probably want somewhere that serves food as well just in case you or your date become too sozzled. Find yourself one of those gastro-pubs. People like those.

- Avoid sports bars and Wetherspoons-esque pubs. People are generally not impressed by those kinds of establishments, although they are easier on the wallet for the serial dater.

- Anyway, give The WestRoom a whirl.

Alternatively, try bowling alleys: always a great idea if you've discovered that you don't have a decent pair of shoes to wear on a date. Get there early and change into the standard bowling pumps and your date will be none the wiser. You will have charmed the pants off of them by the time you leave, so you can change back into your boat shoes.

Also most of them serve booze, so you can get drunk to numb the pain of a socially awkward date.

Also, all of the bowling alleys are miles away from the festival, so you won't run the risk of running into acquaintances if you are a performer type. World of Bowling's probably your man. **Mark Restuccia**

The WestRoom, 3 Melville Place, EH3 7PR. 0131 629 9868, thewestroom.co.uk. Mon-Fri 8.30am-midnight, Sat & Sun 10am-1am. World of Bowling, 11 Newmarket Road, EH14 1RJ. 0131 443 0404, worldofbowling.com. Daily 9am-11pm.

Annual competition bringing you the best musical comedy since 200

'A seemingly bottomless well of musical tale

BRUCE DESSAU, EVENING STANDARD

Entries open every year 1 Oct - 15 De
Live competition January - April

At the Edinburgh Fringe? Come check out the
talent live at the Musical Comedy Awards Showca

www.musicalcomedyawards.co.u
@musicalcomedyuk

Book top musical comedy acts for private

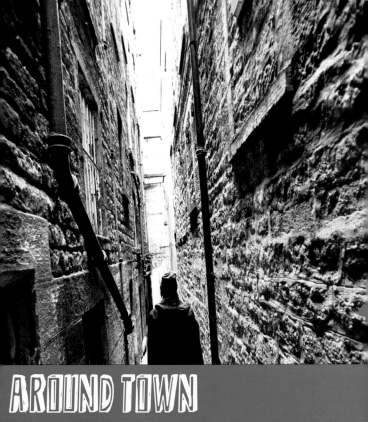

AROUND TOWN

AROUND TOWN

WALKING THE GAUNTLET OF BROKEN DREAMS

// JEFF LEACH //

Since I turned my back on the stereotypical stand-up comic's lifestyle of heavy drinking, soul-destroying womanising and daddy-issue-dodging drug taking, I find myself gazing into the cosmos for a way to feed my debauched soul whilst not breaking the rules of a committed happy relationship. So, so many, ever-changing rules. The way to do so appears to find mirth in the embarrassment of others rather than making yourself the point of interest upon the map of misfortune.

Edinburgh is bursting at the seams with unfortunate souls oozing desperation and most of these appear to congregate in the wings of amateur dramatics. It is within the 'fam of am dram' that I discovered the most successful formula for finding an unforgettable Edinburgh Festival rib-cracker of an adventure. The formula is simple yet brilliant. Simply walk slowly along the Royal Mile, or as it shall henceforth be known, 'The Gauntlet of Broken Dreams'. Here one will find a plethora of pompous, posturing pimple-pressed performers smeared in poorly applied stage make-up and inexpertly sewn costumes, overflowing with bucket-loads of misplaced confidence voraciously spending hours a day thrusting unwanted flyers into your face for their production of 'Schindler's List The Musical' or whatever pap they've decided to peddle that year.

As you meander through this litany of parental let-downs pick the most amateur, irritating, unlikely-to-possess-any-quality-whatsoever of them all, go to their show, and take a small group of friends along. Now here is where the catalyst for comedy comes in. Smuggle in a couple of hip flasks of spirits each and make a group decision to take a large swig every time the action on stage resonates with 'amateur' more than 'dramatics'. By the end of the hour you will have witnessed something more amusing than most of the 'that bloke from Mock The Week' stand-up shows. What's more, the cast will probably be so pleased you have attended AND stayed in your seat for the entire duration of the performance that you will have brought happiness to some of the most sensitive souls at this emotionally and financially draining festival of arts.

You're a giver my friend, and thespians are ready to receive—now take a bow.

LEBENSMÜDE

Just outside Parliament Square, about halfway up the Royal Mile, there is a bronze statue of Adam Smith. Smith is posed resting his hand on 'a globe placed atop a beehive'—which from any real distance looks more like his robot best friend—and with a severe frown (to be expected as he spends all year outside in Scottish weather with birds shitting on his face).

As Smith is the father of free market economics, the statue is the best place to go to pay tribute to rising ticket prices, rising cider prices, the poor quality of rail infrastructure on the East Coast mainline— or anything else that's ever had a negative impact on your Fringe experience.

For me, the statue of Adam Smith is the best rest-stop in Edinburgh. There's a six inch-high step around the base – not high enough to be comfortable, but not low enough to actively cause pain – which is a great place to pause and watch the festival happening around you.

There is a good view downhill of the Tron Kirk and the crowds of punters and performers, while the immediate vicinity seems to attract some of the best street performers and some of the worst flyerers of the Mile.

During the Fringe in 2008, an irritating American wearing a gift shop kilt and sporran spent every day aggressively shouting about his show while standing upon a nearby bollard. One day, while I was resting under the statue, I watched him slip off and injure his hip. This year, as it is our first Fringe together, I plan to introduce my fellow Lebensmüde members to my favourite low-squat pitstop, and hope that we will see some equally wonderful things together.

Ed from Lebensmüde

SARAH CAMPBELL
// ACCIDENT AND EMERGENCY - ROYAL MILE //

"Hey, what venue are you on at?" I said, leaning over into the face of the unconscious woman. "You guys really aren't bad."

The Royal Mile in August. Art Ground Zero. I've seen things on this strip, man, I've seen things. I've seen people shouting in bags, I've seen flaming hacky-sacks, I've seen a boy face down in the gutter, ketchup trickling from his ear, clutching in his clawed hand a flyer for a high-school production of The Sound of Music.

It was the third week of the world's largest arts festival, and like my urine, my mind was cloudy and dark orange. I tottered over the cobbles, numb to the arts raging around me.

But what was this? I hadn't seen these people before. Three paramedics were tending to a middle-aged woman who was lying in some kind of faint. The acting wasn't great, and the dialogue seemed drab, but the costumes and props were top-drawer. They had proper reflective NHS logos all over their green jumpsuits, which I noticed didn't contain a single foundation smear, and their bags were stuffed with all manner of tubing, syringes, and defibrillators...were they backed by Mick Perrin?

"Where are your flyers?" I said to a paramedic as he fitted a neck brace. The man glanced at me and looked a bit upset. If you're gonna commit to the fourth wall then do it 100%, I thought.

It was only when the entire street was cleared and the woman was helped to an ambulance that it dawned on me. My mouth fell open and I stopped following them.

"Actual real thing," I mused as I staggered towards Chocolate Soup. "I think I need to go home soon."

COLIN HOULT
// BROUGHTON STREET //

In Edinburgh I am a big fan of the bottom of Broughton Street (not a euphemism). It is where I have stayed for many years and It has an amazing splash of cool cafes and pubs.

Every year I like to start with a vegetarian haggis in the pub at the bottom. But I pathetically can't recall the name. It is a nice one with a red front.

I remember sitting there and chatting about our shows with various Edinburgh chums over the years so it always felt like the beginning of the festival for me.

They often have little bands and drunk people who may well shake your hand or dance about a bit. It is nice. Similarly the Star Bar, which is located in a tiny alleyway nearby, is open 'til late and whose jukebox has a fondness for belching out Nick Cave and the Rolling Stones. Plus it's open late.

There is a great chip shop also on Broughton that does pizzas and rice balls. Actually, it seems to do pretty much everything and anything. You could probably ask for a manatee burger and they would at least point you in the right direction. I would of course never

© Pete Macloed

eat a manatee. I have nothing but the utmost respect for the ocean's 'sea cow'. Up the road is a great breakfast veggie cafe where you can do emailing and desperately try to find favourable mention of your show in the reviews. Also, I very much love that veggie potato shop off the royal mile. You can get mushrooms in cream. That's right. Mushrooms, in cream. On a potato.

There's an ace sci-fi bookshop off Cowgate near the Underbelly, if you like that sort of thing. It looks really posh and not geeky or smelly or anything so you feel for once that society has almost begun to

accept your nerdy kind.

Other than that, I think, just wander everywhere. It's the most beautiful city in the world!

Barony Bar, 81-85 Broughton St, EH1 3RJ. 0131 558 2874. Mon-Thu 11am-midnight. Fri & Sat 11am-1am, Sun 12.30-11.30pm. Star Bar, 1 Northumberland Place, EH3 6LQ. 0131 539 8070, starbar.co.uk. Daily 11am-1am, later during August. Rapido, 77-79 Broughton St, EH1 3RJ. 0131 556 2041, rapidocaffe.co.uk. Daily 4.30pm-1am. For the Baked Potato Shop, see p151 (Aisling Bea). Transreal Fiction, 46 Candlemaker Row, EH1 2QE. 0131 226 6266, transreal.co.uk. Mon-Fri 11am-6pm, Sat 10am-6pm, Sun midday-5pm.

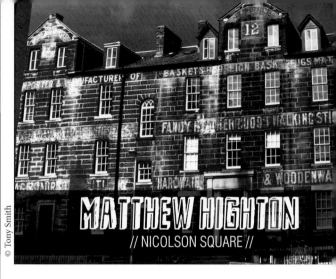

MATTHEW HIGHTON
// NICOLSON SQUARE //

Edinburgh, a cultural hub laced with history, teeming with life on a backdrop of breathtaking architecture, romantic settings and a thousand undiscovered stories. It birthed great names like Arthur Conan Doyle, Eduardo Paolozzi (technically Leith) and Juan Sanchez Vila-Lobos Ramirez of Highlander fame. It's inspired, captivated and left people in awe. There are so many great places to choose from but the one for me is Nicolson Square.

Located roughly somewhere between the North Bridge and Bristo Square, this undiscovered gem housed me for two festivals, hence why it has a firm place in my heart. With its late night disruptions, puddles of sick and a bin haunted by the ghost of an 18th century poet, Nicolson Square offers a wealth of cultural significance. But only by living there can you really understand its baffling beauty. If you get the chance, try and stay in one of its many student houses and watch in the light of the full moon as the grassy area at its centre sinks, revealing a portal to hell, dragging unsuspecting drunks into eternal torments layered with intrinsic personal ironies as the screams of a billion lost souls cry for help.

But maybe I'm biased. It holds so many fond personal memories.

This is after all where, on the darkest night of the year, comedian and beard expert Ian Smith managed to launch a potato from our flat—five stories up—straight into my face on the street below. It is where I saw a man arguing with a pigeon at eleven in the morning. The same Nicolson Square where a fresh-faced troupe of Glee enthusiasts slowly over the course of the month went from practising their show outside my window every morning in week one, to shuffling around red-eyed and stinking of booze as their dreams died, leaving a noise I now have bottled in my bedroom.

Nicolson Square, you sonofabitch. I salute you!

RACHEL PARRIS
// ST MARY'S STREET //

A bit of Edinburgh I really like is St Mary's Street, leading onto Jeffrey Street. I stayed on St Mary's Street for three Edinburghs, so it feels a bit like home. When you first arrive at Waverley station, trundling your suitcase behind you, the walk from the back exit of the station up Jeffrey Street and towards St Mary's is a perfect introduction to your festival.

You get greeted by all the posters first ("oooh exciting shows, look at that font!" you might think), then you walk along what feels like the city wall, looking towards the Regents Gardens ("what a lovely view, and how refreshed I feel after my long journey" you may say aloud, if you're feeling eccentric), then you get a baked potato, perhaps with tuna, from Tempting Tatties ("mmm" you will say definitely aloud) then, having walked for just a few steps from your train, you are right in the heart of it: the Royal Mile, the bottom end where you're less likely to get accosted by gold-painted flyer-wielding student clowns.

Then cross the road and you're on St Mary's Street which boasts cafes, vintage shops, and a really nice old pub on the corner, The Waverley.

© Stu Smith UK

GRAINNE MAGUIRE
// THE GRASSMARKET //

My favourite place in Edinburgh is the Grassmarket. Firstly it looks like I'm in Harry Potter, which is a big tick already for me. Will I buy a second-hand book or a wizard's wand?

The possibilities seem endless. Secondly, there is a Christmas decoration shop there open all year round that fills your heart with wonder. What would it be like to work in such a place?

The place feels like stepping into a foreign village; there is a wine merchant and a whisky shop and a place that just sells cheese.

Then there are the vintage shops. I lose my mind in vintage shops in Edinburgh. The combination of having extra time on my hands and the enthusiasm that being away from home brings, I always get my head completely turned and decide from now on I want to wear pre-war tea dresses.

Then there are the little coffee shops. There is no better place in the entire world than a coffee shop in Edinburgh, eating a caramel biscuit slice and reading a newspaper.

I always feel like I am in some classic old film, but then mid-festival I am usually dressed like an extra for Last of The Summer Wine on crack so that might explain things.

COSTUME HA HA

PAUL PIRIE
// THE GRASSMARKET //

The Grassmarket: its cobbled streets and singing tramps... when the sun is out, it feels like you are in another country. There's lots to see, including Armstrongs, the retro clothing store famed for its overpriced second hand clothes, although there is an amazing assortment of wonderful things to try on (and I do purchase the odd item from time to time!)

There is also a chip shop, where I delight in consuming a white pudding supper (which means it comes with chips). The bars are always packed with a worldwide flavour of people, all smiling, laughing and talking loudly. Tables and chairs are set out when it is sunny so you can watch all the different styles of people roaming, be it a juggler, lawyer, policeman or an American couple arguing about directions.

All this, and behind you there is a mountain that morphs into a castle which is just a stone's throw away from the ladies who dance on tables for £20! (just guessing!) in what the locals call the Pubic Triangle.

It is also near the main comedy venues during the Fringe but not as hectic and loud as some places. The best thing to do is turn your mobile off, take your eyes away from the ground and look up at the beautiful Victorian-era buildings and revel in the architecture long gone from most places. For me it is an escape from modern Britain and everyday life...just for a few hours.

SUSAN CALMAN

© Francisco Diez

// ARCHITECTURE OF NEW TOWN //

In 2011 I stayed in the New Town for the first time. It was extraordinary. As is often the case at the festival I was coming back to the flat early in the morning, when the sun was coming up. As a confirmed Glaswegian I thought little could be more beautiful than a sunrise over my home city, but seeing the New Town early in the morning is extraordinary.

The architecture is superb, solid yet delicate. Behind each window you imagine a professor or an artist is

thinking great thoughts. I noticed a lot of the men seemed to wear corduroy trousers. I wanted to buy corduroy trousers so I could fit in. I wanted to hang out in the coffee shops with them talking about poetry and art and politics. I wanted to eat in the little restaurants and drink wine and be intellectual. In a strange way staying in the New Town made me want to be an entirely different person.

I'm not staying there this year. I haven't bought cords yet.

TOM BELL
// MAGIC TUNNEL //

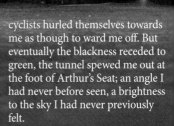

The Edinburgh you see before you is not the only Edinburgh. It is a borrowed city floating on ancient waters. For underneath the sprawling posters and broken dreams breathes the old, Ever Edinburgh. Like a river diverted underground it gracefully makes way every August but even now it still runs silently beneath us and, just occasionally, it breaks surface. It can be hard to spot at first. Perhaps because we of the Edinburgh of August don't want to believe it exists, perhaps because Ever Edinburgh chooses to remain hidden from us. But slow your pace, cast your eyes from the paper stars and gaudy smiles and you might just see it glide past you.

Who is that clean man in a suit boarding a bus as you stagger over South Bridge at 6am? Did you see? A woman with a Farmfoods bag? Where is she headed? I tell you friend, she is headed for the magic tunnel, the only certain path between the two worlds.

After 12 years in the Edinburgh of August I thought I knew it all, but in 2012, at the tail end of the powerful summer of sport, I found myself at the mouth of a tunnel I never knew existed. Along 517 dark metres cyclists hurled themselves towards me as though to ward me off. But eventually the blackness receded to green, the tunnel spewed me out at the foot of Arthur's Seat; an angle I had never before seen, a brightness to the sky I had never previously felt.

As I strolled back towards town I began to perceive things, new things. I became aware of the old names, lost to memory of the Edinburgh of August. I saw now that the Gilded Balloon was a construct built into ancient other words. Like a half remembered dream we whisper 'Teviot' but know its true meaning is lost to us. We stand beneath the belly of the cow and imagine we have heard the sounds of skateboards rattling stone edges yet when we turn, they are gone. But this day, in Ever Edinburgh, I saw it all, and as I walked I learnt of other ways. The desolate caves of the Underbelly are given back to the smugglers and bandits who menace the wealthy travellers of Cowgate. The confused pomp of the Assembly Rooms gives way to a man buttering bread. Food is cheaper in this Edinburgh, the weather, slightly better. They steal the sun for themselves. The Bedlam survives, of course. A rare constant between these two shifting worlds, kept open only by a perpetual, bloody sacrifice of improv. In this world, the penguins run the zoo. I do not make this recommendation lightly, but this tunnel does exist. Should you wish to walk it yourself, strike out from the Pleasance towards St Leonard's Street, they will try and dazzle you with a Homebase but you must be strong and resist. Turn left and weave your way through suburbia towards Pollock Halls, a nestling ground for students and vagabonds. Hidden from view in an unassuming cul-de-sac, waits the Innocent Railway tunnel, a name lost to us in the Edinburgh of August. Burrowed deep into the ground, it broods, waiting to share its secrets.

BEN VAN DER VELDE
// FLESHMARKET CLOSE //

The finest five minutes of the Edinburgh Festival are when I step off the train, breathe in the warm, welcoming musk of hops on the air and imagine the three-and-a-half-week carnival of woozy revelry and nonsense-mongering I have ahead of me. And then I realise I have to drag a suitcase, a rucksack, a laptop, a guitar and most of my worldly possessions up the vertiginious lanes that lead to the Royal Mile. Every year since I first came to Edinburgh it has felt like a welcoming right of passage to forgo taxis, or even the gentle ascent of Cockburn Street, and instead begin the festival with my finest Sherpa Tenzing impression as I lug my sweaty self up the hundreds of slippy steps of Fleshmarket Close.

In any other city, this would be the sort of disreputable back alley that was the sole reserve of tramps and junkies. Not Edinburgh though. Fleshmarket Close is home to two pubs: the Jingling Geordie and the brilliantly named Halfway House, both tempting and mocking weary mountaineers at the same time. I've only ever stopped off on my ascent once, in the Halfway, and was greeted with warm hospitality, soothing whisky and a faint air of 'you're not from round these parts' threat. As a distillation of the Scottish experience, it's perfect. But my favourite part of ascending the Close is at the end.

After trudging up a wet, grey, steep tunnel you are suddenly greeted with the cornucopia of colour, noise and expectation of the Royal Mile. It's like Fleshmarket Close is the birth canal that I have to crawl up to reach the bright light of the Edinburgh festival. Every single year I've made my journey up the Close, by the time I get to the top I'll have bumped into a comic I know—whether it's an open spot or a seasoned headliner—readying themselves for the fray of Edinburgh. I guess they're my comedy midwife, delivering me into the world of the Fringe, not with a slap round the chops and a piece of sharp surgical weaponry, but always with a warm embrace, a freshly-minted Fringe story and an offer of the first pint of the month. They never carry my cases though.

JOHN ROBINS
// A WALK FROM HOME TO VENUE //

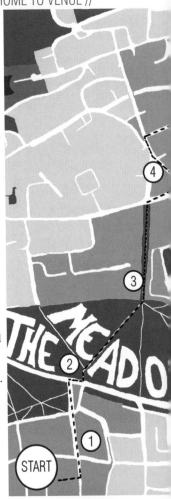

I step out on to Marchmont Road, past the Black Medicine Coffee Company (1) where we went in 2010 when the internet was down, where I sat and SMOKED FAGS when I used to smoke, and where I once told a friend something I had done that I thought was terrible and he just burst out laughing and it was all immediately, wonderfully okay.

And then on to The Meadows, past the new-age Pavilion Cafe (2) where children play so completely in their own worlds, as their mums and dads eat soya milk and coconut husks or somesuch. And then through the Meadows, pausing to watch a few seconds of a cricket match, and I'm starting to feel the buzz! THE BUZZ!

I'll get a coffee from the little stand before Middle Meadow Walk (3) where I once heard the most amazing Spanish guitarist busking. And then past the first posters and billboards I've seen. And I will wonder why anyone would describe something as 'laugh-out-loud funny', and then I'll put Paradise City on my iPod as I start to walk through the people on Teviot Place and everything

FINISH

becomes a montage in my head, and the adrenaline begins to pump and I feel part of it.

After all those months of driving alone, of gigging in the middle of nowhere or feeling totally consumed by crowds in London, for one month of the year I feel part of something! Then past the Bedlam Theatre (4) where I once went in 1998, five years before I first saw live comedy and down Chambers Street (5), THERE IT IS! MY POSTER! HAHA! Look at me there! OH NO SOMEONE'S PUT A COCK ON IT! Oh well…

Then I'll meet someone I kind of know and welcome them like an old friend and ask all about their show because it is before that question has lost all meaning. And I'll get to the Courtyard, or the Caves, and realise I have absolutely no reason to be there other than to feel alive and part of the best working holiday on Earth.

And no matter how much bullshit is to follow, egos and industry and jostling and quotes and reviews and profile, nothing can take away from the fact that we are all here to make people laugh!

STEPHEN CARLIN
// LYING ON THE MEADOWS //

When I was just a kid my Dad would take me and my brothers to see the aeroplanes at Edinburgh Airport. What can I say? I was a cheap date.

In those days there was a viewing gallery to watch the planes and, for an extra five pence, you could operate a pair of binoculars that gave no better view than your own eyes.

Thanks to the new fangled invention of international terrorism the viewing gallery has long since closed down.

> *"I am starting to thin[k] this international terrorism ain't such a good thing..."*

(Personally I am starting to think this international terrorism ain't such a good thing. I mean when you start pissing on my childhood memories Al Qaeda, you have gone too far!)

I suppose if I genuinely wanted respite from the madness of the Fringe I would try and recreate my childhood and visit the viewing gallery. Sadly that option no longer exists.

So the best I can do is lie in the Meadows on a clear sunny day (I think you may already have spotted the flaw in my plan) and gaze at the aeroplanes far above and wonder: with the biggest arts festival in the world in Edinburgh, why are these losers flying abroad?

PETER BUCKLEY HILL
// WEDNESDAY //

There are three dimensions of space and one of time. And perhaps there are others, curled in fractal balls of string-theory string.

(When I was a wolf cub, Akela told us always to carry a clean white handkerchief and a piece of string. Presumably in case we needed to surrender and build a new universe.)

So, when the editor asked me my favourite place in Edinburgh, I said Wednesday. Time is a place. And a website named Such Small Portions ought to appreciate fundamental particles, especially in the home of Higgs.

But in a four-coordinate system, Wednesday isn't enough. We have x, y and z axes, as well as t. Especially if you're doing this in conjunction with Google Maps, on which Wednesday is notoriously difficult to plot.

My favourite place in Edinburgh, during the Fringe, is on the top of a bus going to somewhere I don't know, on a Wednesday.

Wednesday is my day off. Six days shalt thou labour, and I do. Six days I answer every silly question in the universe. Well, apart from string-related ones. The Free Fringe is my invention and obsession, and although I never discovered the Higgs Boson, I discovered one truth about performers: if you give them something for nothing, they'll want more for less.

Them? Us. I'm one.

And so on Wednesdays you will find me (though I hope you don't) on the top deck of a randomly chosen Lothian bus, clutching my £3.50 day ticket, going to somewhere I haven't been before, and coming back from the same place.

GRAHAM FELLOWS
// A MIXTURE OF QUIET PLACES //

Edinburgh during the festival is a nightmare. People everywhere. I don't mind having lots of heaving bodies in my shows. But when I'm not performing, I deliberately seek the quieter, less-trodden byways that make the madness disappear for a while.

And there are surprisingly many of them, even in the city centre. Naming these places isn't easy, as I have never noted their precise location—I have just felt that I have got away from the crazy circus that is the Fringe, and tasted normality for a few minutes.

One of these spots is when you turn off the Royal Mile on to Jeffrey Street and the sound of bagpipes and yabbering tourists fades suddenly, to be replaced by a gust of autumnal wind whipping along the buildings, and you pass a lone Edinburgh resident hurrying back to the office after their lunch break.

Another is as you walk down some steps into a basement French restaurant near St George's Square when it is about to close and you have the place to yourself.

Last year I discovered the beach at Portobello with my girlfriend, Geraldine. There were swans and we befriended a Sri Lankan couple from North Wales who were visiting a poorly relative. The festival wasn't mentioned once.

And then there was the Moscow State Circus out of town somewhere. I took my son, George, and we rode on a double-decker bus that was packed with normal Edinburgh folk – sitting there in silence, musing on their day. No brightly coloured cagoules or bumbags. No festival brochures being unfolded and frantically studied.

Edinburgh and the Fringe will always be in my heart, especially those strange, hard-to-find—but unmistakable once in them—out-of-the-way places.

GREG PROOPS
CAFE ROYAL // CAFE ST HONORE // THE GRAIN STORE

I have a few hideouts in E'bro. First, no-one from the festival goes to the Leith. You can have fancy fine food or go for chips and groove on the sea gulls and shippy atmosphere.

Calton Hill at night is a groovy place to see the lights and dig the after-dark skyline. If you want to be very alone, walk through the Princes Street Gardens and go to the cemetery down the end; the headstones are fascinating, and you will find solitude.

The Cafe Royal is known to all, but if you get there early for lunch you can have the whole joint to yourself and gorge on oysters. Heaven.

Cafe St Honore is a great place for a long lunch and to watch esteemed members of Parliament do some day drinking.

There is also the Grain Store in the Grassmarket, a hippie-ly run place of farm-to-gun-to-table awesome. I made everyone try my peppered venison liver. Everyone loved it. You heard me.

Sometimes plain sight is the best place to hide. Walk the Royal Mile from the castle down to Holyrood; it thins out the lower you go and there are wild, hidden pubs and tea houses all along the way.

One year on the Mile at a cutesy-pie tea place, the charming proprietress, a woman of maturity, told us of a drinks party she attended where a friend had a heart attack and expired.

Rather than stop the fun, she explained they stowed him in the boot of her car and kept drinking.

It was no use taking him to hospital as he was 'deed'.

The perfect Edinburgh ending to a charming stroll and lovely cakes.

TIERNAN DOUIEB
// PENGUIN PARADE AT EDINBURGH ZOO //

Edinburgh Zoo, EH12 6TS. 0131 334 9171, edinburghzoo.org.uk.
Summer hours daily 9am-6pm.

AROUND TOWN

Who likes penguins? Not the biscuits. The other ones. You know, with little black jackets and the waddling.

Not the biscuits, no. You know, the ones that are birds but can swim and not fly. You know? The ones from Happy Feet?

No, not the biscuits. Ok, you have a biscuit. Now let's talk about actual penguins.

In the corner of Edinburgh (it's not actually the corner, but I I feel that describes it better than just saying 'that bit of Edinburgh') is Edinburgh Zoo. Luckily someone with incentive put Edinburgh Zoo in Edinburgh, which is good news for everyone involved.

Aside from a menagerie of wee beasties and not-so-wee beasties and beasties that wee, Edinburgh Zoo's most excellent of features can only be the penguin parade at 2.15pm everyday.

Yes, penguins. Yes, parading. No, not the biscuits. And no, sadly they don't have batons or hats or do jazz hands. Neither does one have a trumpet nor a drum. Don't be all sad.

Yes it would be better with all of those things, but I think you will be surprised at just how wonderfully entertaining some tiny beaked butlers all shimmying towards you can be. Hella entertaining.

That's how much. I used a word that isn't even a word.

There is a chance that due to the weather the parade may not happen, but remember they are used to wet weather and ice, which makes it unlikely. It also explains why they are happy enough to parade in Edinburgh, a place that not only isn't a stranger to such weather, but gives that weather sweets and puppies without concern from anyone else.

There is a higher chance that not all the penguins will take part. Some days they all march like a mini-army; other days just one or two scouts are sent out on recon while the rest hide within the barracks.

Yes, it is far more enjoyable if you pretend they are all bird soldiers. Or professional dancers. Or giant weebles. It's up to you, those are just a few of my favourites.

So escape the hustle bustle and grab a bus to see what I think is easily always the best show in town. I will be there enjoying my day off with some nature-based humour and my Penguin biscuits.

© Edinburgh Dungeons

SUZY BENNETT
// EDINBURGH DUNGEONS //

The Edinburgh Dungeon, 31 Market St, EH1 1DF. 0871 423 2250, thedungeons.com/edinburgh. Festival hours daily 10am-7pm.

Situated conveniently right next to Waverley Station is the Edinburgh Dungeons. I have visited the London version several times and learned all about Sweeney Todd and Jack the Ripper and other 'Londony' horrors (you know, like Boris Johnson and that) and its always a good giggle with friends. I managed to avoid the tiresome, long queues and pricey entrance fee as I was the lucky holder of a free pass due to working for the same company, oh yeah, check ME out!

So during my first stay in Edinburgh back in 2007, I would of course want to check out the Scottish version of live action Horrible Histories led by ambitious young actors in face paints. It is a fun day out and you learn stuff too. I was curious as to what legends Scotland's Dungeon tour would unveil (would there be a Rab C Nesbitt section I wondered? Would I be forced to watch The Krankies whilst being circled by zombies?)

During the month of August there is a surprising lack of tourists lining up outside to enter the mysterious building with the bloody red writing and flaming torches on the walls. (It's almost as if something else is happening in the town to divert entertainment seekers away!)

My friend and I decided to have a few hours away from the chaos of the festival and find a safe haven where we could escape for a while and learn some history and be entertained by some enthusiastic BTEC-trained actors who would definitely not try to flyer us.

The tour takes you in a group around dimly-lit passages as you encounter a torturer demonstrating tongue pulling out and castration devices on unlucky volunteer (I enjoyed this part as I was experiencing some 'man issues', so noted down some tips).

You are told the stories of Burke and Hare (sadly Simon Pegg was not available for this part), the legend of Sawney Bean, and you get lost in a labyrinth of mirrors and taken on a scary boat ride to your 'doom'.

There are impressive special effects and lots of frights and surprises and gross-out gags. William Wallace and Mary King's ghost were particularly impressive and state of the art. I had such a great giggle the first time that I returned last year with a colleague from my show as we had some time to kill before our trains home. We were hungover and had just eaten a large breakfast, so the quick drop ride really was a risky venture, but we were brave. The souvenir keyrings of our terrified faces as we were dropped from a height in the dark, my hair styled in electric shock chic, is a memento I shall treasure.

(Although I only bought them as I had a discount.)

We laughed and interacted from start to finish and pretended not to be scared, and it was a nice way to round off our Edinburgh. I heartily recommend a visit to this interesting place if you are not too much of a scaredy cat. Don't forget to take your sense of humour and possibly a Tena Lady for the 'jumpy bits'.

On an unrelated note, it is MEANT to smell of wee down there as it is 'authentic'.

PS should I write 'urine' instead of 'wee' as this means small up here, right?

PPS have I put people off by talking about urine too much?

MICK PERRIN

// MALCOLM HARDEE //

My first Edinburgh was, I think, 1982: mostly outside, usually wet, with the street busking act Pookiesnackenburger (later STOMP), along with busking legends JJ Waller and Tim Batt, and of course not forgetting the incredible Cliff Hanger Theatre Company. My job was to help with the production, and of course to help 'bottle' the audience before heading off to Bannermans on Cowgate to count up the proceeds and split the day's takings.

During one of these sessions I was seconded to something that was (I was assured) going to be a great laugh. Whatever it was, it was taking place on the Lothian Road and I had to do something when told to do so. The man doing the thing that would make me laugh was Malcolm Hardee, who I had never met before...though I knew of his infamy.

The skit was to be performed in front of the press corps at the official opening of the Fringe festival. I handed Malcolm a crate to stand on and, after clapping loudly several times, he finally brought the happy, care-free assembly of press-people and festival dignitaries to a hushed silence. "Ladies and gentleman. It is with heavy heart that I have been nominated with the terrible task of informing you all that the wonderful, talented and beautiful Glenda Jackson has been killed in a car accident on the way to the festival."

As the audience began to discuss the news between themselves, some openly crying, Malcolm continued with his soliloquy to Miss Jackson. Then, as arranged, he gave me a nod and I handed him a piece of paper. Malcolm once again brought the crowd to a hushed silence.

"Ladies and gentleman, I have just been handed important news. It appears that it was Brenda Jackson that was killed in the car accident, not Glenda. So, carry on enjoying yourselves." With that the mood of the audience changed and we both legged it as fast as we could.

Whenever I go past the spot on the Lothian Road where this all took place, I say a little prayer to the memory of Malcolm Hardee. Happy days.

CHRIS DANGERFIELD
// METHODIST CHURCH //

Every time I go to the festival I visit this room. It's only of use to me for one and a half hours every Tuesday from 1pm in the afternoon. So that's three visits, four and a half hours in total. Being an atheist the rest of the building is not only of no use to me, I find it offensive and complicit. I shuffle past rooms full of whispers and tread polished staircases lined with posters about The Lord.

This room at those times is quite different. I go alone but meet around 15 to 20 other people there. I don't know them, but I know some of the places they have been. I know their anguish, their guilt and their shame. I know their battles and the successes; I know their failures and the dust that threatens to settle around their dreams. We share a fear but exchange a hope. We give it to each other, and anyone else who may want it. In this room we learn acceptance.

In this room back, lovers of a self lost sometimes The beauty holding out a out their hand distress get the freedom is on out into the lives are saved, children get their parents start loving again. The incredible violence in loathing, fear, resentment and loss is reversed, transformed and overcome. and heartbreaking charm of one human hand to a stranger, and a stranger holding to another. In this room, humans in opportunity to reclaim their futures; a offer, it is multiplied and taken back world.

The grin, a sleepless cleaning ammonia of superiority. reflection, a a moment of growth, a of love. odd cackle from a toothless tears slowly rolling down expression; the faint smell of products jostling with the light slightly pissy trousers for nasal All this, a moment of moment of identification, of humanity, a moment moment, essentially,

49

STUART GOLDSMITH

// LOCATION X //

Chambers St, EH1 1JF. 0300 123 6789, nms.ac.uk. Daily 10am-5pm.

Look, I'm not just going to give you this one on a plate, OK? This is simultaneously: the best view from within the city; a place of calm and reflection just seconds away from the hubbub; and a genuine secret. I don't want it cluttered up with seekers, looters and dungeoneers, so you're going to have to prove yourself worthy. Work it out from these fiendish clues, or STAY AWAY.

My first is in 'roof garden at the top of the National Museum of Scotland' but not in 'jjwzzzyk'. My second is also in 'roof garden at the top of the National Museum of Scotland' but not in 'cccB∆∆'. Likewise my third to forty-seventh. Solve the riddle, and begin your quest...

Upon arrival at the public bit, the bit that looks like the Klingon Embassy, you first need to outwit the guards. One of them always tells the truth, the other has a hat. The correct question is: "If I asked the other one, who would he say is the one with the hat?"

They mull it over; you dash past. Entrance is free, donations welcome.

Next find the lift. It is very easy at this stage to enter the decoy lift, which simply moves visitors up and down between floors. Don't be a sap—instead use the lift which

© National Museum Scotland

has no indication that it goes somewhere special.

It's worth asking one of the staff. They would die before they admitted your goal actually exists, but it's fun to demand directions outright, and watch their face freeze in a spasm of plausible deniability.

Lift, stairs, corridor, stairs again, outside for a bit, corridor again, stairs. Only the penitent man shall pass... And out into the sunlight! If you're lucky.

Breathe in the mountain herb-garden, enjoy a view to parallel Arthur's Seat just seconds from the bustle of the city, tot up your gold pieces, and marry the mayor's daughter. YOUR ADVENTURE ENDS HERE.

BARRY FERNS
// CAMERA OBSCURA AND THE WORLD OF ILLUSIONS/

Camera Obscura and World of Illusions, Castlehill, Royal Mile, EH1 2ND. 0131 226 3709, camera-obscura.co.uk. Daily 9.30-9pm.

One of the funnest and funniest things I do, when the long Edinburgh days and nights make me weary to the bone, is to go up to the Royal Mile—almost as far as the castle but not quite—and visit Edinburgh's Camera Obscura.

It is a rare working instrument and is about 150 years old. The camera itself is amazing if you haven't seen it before. And it is interesting to find out about the city and get a good idea of the history of Edinburgh. I always take people there if they are new to the festival.

But the best part of it (for me) is that there are a few Explainers there. They are usually brilliantly bad actors (the proper title of the place is The Camera Obscura and the World of Illusions! and the whole thing is so over the top). They really overact their part and try to make it all fun and interesting for people and kids. They are always totally and unintentionally funny.

It almost feels like you're in a comedy sketch, but you're not. This is real life, the life...of the camera obscura!! (Ooooh!)

Edinburgh is a beautiful place, with stone-cobbled streets, where every building looks like a castle. Especially Edinburgh Castle. It looks heaps like a castle. But, if I have one tip for anyone travelling to Edinburgh Castle this year, it's this: pay the admission. The site of the Edinburgh Tattoo, the castle thrives with tourists daily, all wishing to explore the dark halls and almost-ancient artefact-filled rooms to get a taste of what life was like when kings ruled the land, and nobody knew what a toothbrush was. And with line-ups for castle entry tickets seemingly a Royal Mile long, we decided that we'd have to do a whirlwind tour of the castle, sans tickets...Yep. We tried to sneak into a building that was specifically designed so that it would be impossible to sneak into. Needless to say, our tour of this historic icon started, and ended, in the gift shop. Don't make the same mistake I did. Pay the admission. In advance! God bless the internet. MATT OKINE

Edinburgh Castle, EH1 2NG, 0131 225 9846, edinburghcastle.gov.uk, Daily 9.30am-

VENUE TALES

ED BARTLAM

// UNDERBELLY //

The Underbelly down in Cowgate opened in 2000 after I got permission from the council as a rather naive 19-year-old to open the venue, took a tiny bit of money, and that's how it was born.

The comedy only really started in 2002 but over the years we've had anyone and everyone: Russell Howard, Alex Zane and Jerry Sadowitz.

Jerry once did the late show, and before he went on, he said he was going to try and see how many people he could get to leave the room. He got the entire audience to leave bar about four people just by being so brutal with them. But then he did another year with us at Underbelly and two years at the Cow doing close-up magic, and the second year there was one of the best shows I've ever seen.

Later, in 2006, we had the big moment in our growth, opening the cow in Bristo Square. My business partner, Charlie Wood, and I were out for drinks with Priorité A Gauche, and we were telling them the plans for the tent. One of them said, if you're building a tent, you need to put a head, legs and udders on it. So we can't lay claim to the cow tent idea but we're glad we went out for drinks that night!

Now we're up to 15 rooms, from 50-seaters to the 1000-seat McEwan Hall. However for those who like intimacy with their stand-up comedy, the 120-seat Dairy Room is lovely—we had Susan Calman and Felicity Ward in there.

We've got dozens of memories from the Underbelly but one I remember well was when Stewart Lee closed Spank, and he had a heckler. If there's anyone you don't heckle, it's him. The guy had seen his set before and gave away the punchline to a typical Lee joke. The whole room went silent and Stewart just said, in his very quiet way: "who was that?" This guy put his hand up, and Stewart said: "I want you to come on stage...right now...and say sorry. Not just to me, I want you to say sorry to the audience." This guy was completely wrecked by the end.

ELEANOR CONWAY

My favourite place during the chaotic and fiscally crippling month of Edinburgh is a bastion of calm in the flurry of beer and beer goggles that engulf Bristo Square: the green room of my 2012 and 2013 venue, the Wee Coo at the Underbelly.

Set in the midst of a thriving and often raucous and lairy bar in Bristo Square, the green room is separated from the Wee Coo's stage by a curtain and door. It is a calm, tranquil gateway to debauchery and 'get your tits out' craziness of the stag and hen dos outside.

I had the gruelling slot of midnight last year with my show Comedy Rumble and so my working day would start in the early evening, sorting flyers out in the green room, all the while trying to keep super-quiet while I listened to the Northern lilts of Paul McCaffery and the feisty Canadian punchlines of Dana Alexander. I have heard both of their 2012 shows many,

> *"You don't know if your numbers are reflective of you, your show, the weather or the ongoing turmoil in Sudan..."*

many times (you should check them both live if you get the chance) but in micro-snippets and in completely different order, so for me my recollection of both shows is a bit scrambled. It is a bit like dropping a completed Scrabble board and trying to reassemble the game.

Promoting Comedy Rumble without an agent, promoter or producer has been a very lonely job. Everyone has bad days, and even though Bristo Square is an entertainment hub, at particularly slow periods you don't know if your numbers are reflective of you, your show, the weather or the ongoing turmoil in Sudan. It gave me comfort and confidence to be able to gauge density of laughs from Dana and Paul's show which occupied the two slots before mine in order to suss out what the day's crowds were like.

Don't get me wrong, that green room was the scene of great preparation and excitement for me: the show days where we had Jarred Christmas and Mick Foley waiting to come onto Comedy Rumble, my first sell-out night and my subsequent first five-star review. The results have seen the show sell out at The Comedy Cafe in London and get staged at members' club Soho House and London's infamous landmark, the Gherkin.

That green room, a place that only exists for a month in August, is to me a place to set your game face, to justify to yourself the worst business model in the world, to be able to re-centre and repackage that brash confidence to go out there with sass, and sell a show to a bunch of drunk revellers who may or may not urinate mid-show.

To hope to set in stone another Edinburgh success story, of which the end is yet to come.

ANNIE MCGRATH
// UNDERBELLY - COWGATE //

I spend eleven months a year looking forward to Edinburgh, but when I am there, I want to crawl into a dark hole. That is why I have chosen the dark corners of Underbelly as my favourite place.

The Underbelly seats are an excellent place for a mid-flyering nap: damp and in the shadows. If you time it well, you can also avoid seeing or speaking to anyone.

On a rainy day (most days) or a beautifully sunny day (never), it is the perfect (absolutely fine) place to retreat from the Mile, drink a warm pint of tap water and ask yourself, "what are we all doing and why are we all doing it (again)?" I do love the Fringe, but... know what I mean?

ANTHONY ALDERSON
// THE PLEASANCE //

Jump in a cab and simply ask for the Pleasance Courtyard. Described once as the centre of the cultural universe, no visit to Edinburgh is quite complete without a little dose of something Pleasance!

The Pleasance may be slightly off the beaten track, but once you find it, you will almost certainly want to stay a while. The theatre programme is seductive, the comedy raucous and the drama often life-changing.

Entering the bottom archway at 60 The Pleasance is like entering a secret garden. It is an explosion of life, full of the most astonishing surprises and where the atmosphere is legendary. It is little wonder that some of the world's best and well-loved actors, directors and comedians are drawn to one of the Pleasance Courtyard's 16 stages to perform.

Careful where you sit down: you never know who you might sit next to - and if you want to get on TV, just stand in a queue.
Set in what is otherwise a sleepy backwater in the unassuming east end of Edinburgh, the Pleasance is a place to explore and take risks. There are performance spaces crammed into every nook and cranny, and just when you think you have got to the end, you'll find there is another corner, another cobbled courtyard, and yet more excitement.

You could spend the whole month at the Pleasance and still not see everything on offer. If after a day at the Courtyard you don't feel you've quite had enough, well, five minutes up the road in Bristo Square is the Pleasance Dome. And if you know the right person to ask—and apparently that's all you have to do—you might even get into the infamous Brooke's Club, a haven for the stage-weary performers that stays open until 5am in the morning every night of the festival.

MILTON JONES

Like the topography of the city, the Edinburgh Fringe is full of highs and lows for every comedian. We all have a love-hate relationship with the place: the best of times, the worst of times, or more likely, the worst of reviews in the Times. The hills and the beer, the cobbles and the queues; permanently excited and bored at the same time, and always the sound of bagpipes in the background.

But there is a strange little chamber under the Pleasance Courtyard—that ceases to be a corridor when both fire doors swing shut—just after the stairs and before you get to the Gents. Isolated for a few seconds as you pass through, you can briefly be all alone and yet surrounded by the plastered posters of years gone by: the famous looking younger, as well as lots of emblazoned names you've never heard of.

But all these shows, both good and bad, are without exception long forgotten, their exaggerated promises and wacky faces overlapping and peeling at the edges. In those brief seconds of solitude there is a chance to remember that whatever extreme you are experiencing at the time, it is entirely temporary, so best try and not take it all too seriously.

Then a door swings open and a friend comes through. "Good show tonight, many in?" The room has disappeared, and it is a corridor once more and just a means of getting to somewhere else.

But whether you are on your way up or down, it is good to take that balancing moment in what can be a quite literally sobering little purgatory.

WILLIAM BURDETT-COUTTS
// ASSEMBLY //

We started running the Assembly Rooms in 1981 when the stand-up comedy world that we now know didn't really exist. Comedy on the Fringe was more about revue groups from Oxford or Cambridge, or alternative comedy.

I always think that today's comedy really began with the birth of Channel 4, which suddenly spawned interest in comedy from the TV world. A host of great names like French and Saunders, John Sessions, Hugh Laurie and Stephen Fry, Griff Rhys Jones, Lenny Henry, Rory Bremner and Angus Deayton kicked off their comedy socks and trod the boards of the Assembly Rooms before huge careers in television. Graham Norton went from doing a one-man show in a 100-seat venue to being a TV star in a year.

Assembly no longer runs the Assembly Rooms—after 30 years our tenure there came to an end and we have moved to a new world based around George Square but we have taken with us our comedy tradition and great names still abound, from Adam Hills and Milton Jones to David Baddiel and Rich Hall.

Are there stories from over the years? Of course. I remember a promoter trying to persuade me to put an unknown comedian onto the stage of the Music Hall—our biggest theatre at the time—and I was very sceptical. It was Peter Kay.

Similarly, Eddie Izzard turned up at my office one day in Camberwell, London, straight out of university and wanted a big space. I turned him down. Did I ever regret that!

The Fringe is truly part of comedy legend and new faces join us every year. I've no doubt at the coming festival we will all be wowed by someone new. I once saw Tim Minchin in a comedy line-up in Australia and he instantly wanted to go onto a big stage, although no one in Edinburgh knew him. I demurred and took another comedian; Karen Koren very sensibly did take him on and he was an enormous hit. That's the Fringe!

KAREN KOREN
// GILDED BALLOON //

The Gilded Balloon became my life from 1986, though it very much crept up on me. I started it with actor and comedian friends in mind. The new alternative comedy boom was big down south, but was still relatively new in Scotland.

These friends wanted to perform in Edinburgh at the Fringe and had difficulty finding venues; there were plenty of church halls and a couple of professional venues, but none that specialised in comedy.

The Gilded Balloon was born, the growth of the venue was rapid, and by 1987 Late 'n' Live began; the first late night hang out for comedians, where stand-ups lived or died on stage nightly during the Fringe, and their fellow comics watched and heckled as much as the audiences. In 1988 So You Think You're Funny?, the stand-up competition for newcomers who have only worked in the business for one year or less, started. Through this competition emerged some of the most important new stand-ups in the last 27 years.

It was by the late eighties and early nineties that the Gilded Balloon was taken seriously within the industry, with more and more emerging talent. Comedy became big business and it also became incredibly competitive. It was hard to keep up. Gilded Balloon prided itself on the personal touch, staying smaller than its competitors. The staff, management and I in particular enjoyed a more family-style approach to the running of our business.

Consequently many friendships have been made over the years between staff and performers alike, many of whom have gone on to sparkling careers within the entertainment industry. I am personally very proud of the history of the Gilded Balloon and there are far too many people who have had their first helping hand through us. My personal friends who I keep in touch with and see as often as I can are Jo Brand, Bill Bailey, Tim Minchin, Jenny Eclair, Dylan Moran, Ardal O'Hanlon, and there are many more.

NEW ART CLUB
// ONE-WOMAN LUNCHTIME SHOWS //

Whilst in Edinburgh my favourite place is not actually one place but various places around the city at a particular time of day: lunchtime. It has, however, nothing to do with eating.

Every year I scour the pages of the Fringe brochure looking for one-woman shows with one thing in common. Before you jump to conclusions, it is not the promise of nudity or erotic entertainment. My perversion is much worse.

The thing that I am looking for, as I read the blurb, is something that sounds like it might touch the right spot, unscrew my internal stop cock and allow salty water to pour down my face in a dark room full of strangers. The shows can usually be found between 12.30 and 2.30pm.

This is the perfect lunchtime tonic, placing my own personal misery (brought on by very Edinburgh-focused events: not selling enough tickets or not receiving enough stars, or worse, receiving enough stars but still not selling enough tickets, or any combination of these, with added rain) in the wider context of actual life events - unrequited love, love stopped short by war, love made impossible by the demands of everyday life. Occasionally a male performer has done this to me but it has only ever been Daniel Kitson. He is the exception that proves the rule.

As I leave the venue and re-enter the world, I love the feeling of being alone with my emotions in this amazing, bustling city, surrounded by thousands of people who may, for all I know, be doing exactly the same thing; of wanting to find the performer and tell them how much the show affected me but knowing that if I did I would just burst into tears again. Thanks, emotionally wrought one-woman shows. You rule lunchtime Edinburgh.

RHYS JAMES
// PLEASANCE DOME TOILETS //

Every comic needs to find their sanctuary, away from all the shit of the Edinburgh Fringe. For me, that is the Pleasance Dome toilets, amongst all the shit of the Edinburgh Fringe. Being part of the biggest arts festival in the world can be overwhelming and there is a lot to digest.

What better place to do that than in a toilet cubicle? I don't know if it's the solitude, allowing momentary escape from the chaos upstairs, or the constant sound effects, loud and reassuring as if to say 'here, anything goes', but whenever I'm in these toilets I come out feeling relieved.

> *"I find it incredibly relaxing to have a nice sit down, check my emails, read a magazine or sometimes just have a good old think..."*

I have an incredibly fast metabolism, which is why I haven't aged or put on weight since I was 14, so a clean and trustworthy toilet is a necessity for me. Often, I'll be having dinner with a friend during the Fringe, tell them I'm just "popping to the loo" and emerge days later, looking paler and more gaunt than ever. But feeling oddly refreshed.

The Pleasance Dome toilets are nicely decorated, well kept and the right side of 'busy'. I find it incredibly relaxing to have a nice sit down, check my emails, read a magazine or sometimes just have a good old think, before wiping away the blood, pulling up my trousers and getting on with my day.

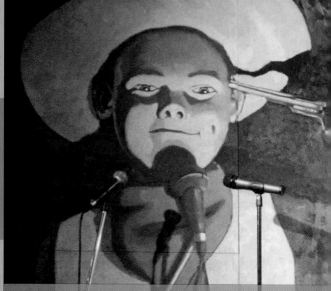

TOMMY SHEPPARD
// THE STAND //

We started The Stand Comedy Club as a hobby back in 1995 in a tiny basement of a pub in Edinburgh's Grassmarket. By 1998 we were running three nights a week in three different pubs. And then I got made redundant. So with the time, money and opportunity to do something completely different we set about turning the hobby into a business.

We're still unlikely and accidental business people even today. Even though the club now has three venues with sisters in Glasgow and Newcastle, the basic idea is the same as it ever was. That idea is to provide a platform for new innovative stand-up and give punters a decent night of thought-provoking entertainment as cheaply as possible.

We do that every night of the week. Over the years we have had pretty much anyone who is anyone in the world of comedy tread our tiny stage. And we have been responsible for getting a few people started too, from Frankie Boyle back in the day to the likes of Kevin Bridges and Gary Tank Commander more recently.

Every Monday for the last 14 years we have run Red Raw, widely regarded as the best open mic night in the UK. Sometimes it's good, sometimes it's bad, and sometimes it's so bad it's good.

This cosy little basement now has its own place in comedy history; quite literally the DNA of some of our finest entertainers is engrained in our walls. It is the only venue on the Fringe, the world's largest arts festival, which is purely dedicated to stand-up and over the years it has become the comedians' favourite hang-out. That's why Alexei Sayle, Stewart Lee, Sarah Millican and dozens more choose to play here, even though they could fill much bigger rooms elsewhere.

© The Stand

SHOPPING

IAN RANKIN
your gap year

LITERATURE
AND OTHER
WELL-KNOW
AUTHORS IN
ALPHABETI
ORDER.

NEXT DOOR
ART · CRAFT · PHOTOGRAPH
ARCHITECTURE · THEATRE · M
MEDIA · FILM · HOBBIES · COOKE
CLASSICS · ARCHEOLOGY · HIST
MILITARY · MARITIME · EXPLORA
SCIENCE · MEDICINE · NAT. HIST
FOREIGN LANGUAGE · REFERENC
MAPS · TRAVEL · SPORT · POLIT
PSYCHOLOGY · SOCIAL SCIENCES
ECONOMICS · OCCULT · ALT. MEDIC
VICTORIAN ILLUSTRATED · GEOGRA

HEALTH AND SAFETY NOTICE
DANGEROUS LADDERS
OPEN THE LADDER FULLY
THANKS TO EDINBURGH CITY COUNCIL

SHOPPING

CASTLE

ABANDOMAN
// RED DOG MUSIC //

Red Dog Music, 1 Grassmarket Edinburgh, Midlothian EH1 2HY 0131 229 8211, reddogmusic.co.uk Mon - Sat: 10am - 6pm Sun: 12pm - 5pm

Whenever I'm near the Grassmarket, I will find myself gradually wandering in the general direction of Red Dog Music, my favourite Edinburgh musical instrument shop.

I love musical instrument shops. I don't really play an instrument. I can play songs by Oasis that I learnt at 17 (bar the ones that include the ambitious 'F chord', my fingers still won't accept that one), and that's about it. When I go in there, my fingers instinctively know what to do - jam out Wonderwall followed by a rough approximation of Don't Look Back in Anger. Truth be told, I never really liked Oasis. I was always more of a hip hop fan, but a friend who taught me only liked Oasis, so this is all I seemed to learn.

The good folks at Red Dog Music will usually chat with me about what tone I'm looking for, what type of guitar I play, and various other musical questions. All this, despite the fact that we can all hear how much I'm struggling to play Wonderwall. Sure, it's the right chords, but it's being played incredibly slowly, like I'm trying to re-appropriate it for a John Lewis ad.

After this, I'll end up attempting to play an electronic drum kit, usually with headphones on. With this, I literally can't play a thing. I know what the various drums do, and what order they're meant to be played in to create a rhythm, but my flailing hands treat drums very much like they do when patting my head and rubbing my stomach at the same time (they seem to be behaving more out of curiosity than co-ordination).

Lastly, I'll nerd over all things computer-music related. Here, I know at least enough to hold a conversation. With computers, no hand-to-eye coordination is needed to play a drumbeat. There are fancy controllers to make it play drums that have been sampled from kits throughout the world. It's hard to sound bad when programming in this section.

I'll usually end up buying something computer-music related, convincing myself that after all the shows, I'll head home and jam a musical masterpiece. I have about 5 pieces of kit from Red Dog and very little music created to support these purchases. That said, I've already checked their website to see what they've got in store for 2013.

BACONFACE

// BACKBEAT RECORDS //

Backbeat Records, 31 East Crosscauseway, EH8 9HE. 0131 668 2666. Mon-Sat 10am-5.30pm.

My first trip to England was last summer, when my fellow Canadians The Lumberjacks gave me a guest spot at The Assembly Rooms. I stumbled across Backbeat records quite by accident when I was out trying to score a decent cup of coffee in your puzzlingly primitive burgh.

Backbeat took me back to my home town – Chilliwack, British Columbia, Canada – in the seventies. Downtown American stoners that had crossed the border and split to the woods to skip the draft sat amidst crates of psychedelic vinyl in tumbledown head shops, and Doogie's pad has that same gold mine ambience.

There's no apparent order to the way this righteous retailer has stacked his stash, but he'll lend you a stepladder to scan the shelves, and somewhere in those muddled palettes of vinyl you know there's the nugget you've spent your whole goddam lifetime looking for.

Last year Backbeat spat a battered original of Ptarmigan's uniquely Canadian acid-folk album right out at me, but I'm still searching for a mint copy of Heritage by the great Ontario psyche-prog band Christmas, and a replacement for my long lost copy of the Vancouver visionary Claire Lawrence's solo debut. Maybe this Summer Backbeat will render them unto me. Here's hopin'. Get your white Scotch asses down to Backbeat, and lay your poonds down on the desk.

TOM ALLEN

// JOHN LEWIS'S TOWEL DEPARTMENT //

John Lewis, St James Centre, EH1 3SP. 0131 556 9121. Mon-Wed, Fri 9am-6pm, Thu 9am-8pm, Sat 9am-6.30pm, Sun 10am-6pm.

SHOPPING

My favourite—and little-known—place in Edinburgh has to be, without doubt, the towel department in John Lewis. There is something about all those neatly-arranged fluffy pastel shades that is intensely calming.

The world's biggest arts festival is a lot of fun but I sometimes worry that there's no escape from the ceaseless posters and flyer teams, the thousands of other performers and the people in the industry known as The Industry. I am never quite sure exactly who these people are but if I meet one I want to make sure I am feeling rested.

I draw huge strength from the fact that none of these will be seeking out something as practical, and perhaps indulgent, as a towel set. Yarn twist? Pima cotton?... Egyptian cotton? Not sure? Ask an assistant, they are very knowledgeable.

You can pass the time of day talking about something that has nothing to do with the festival and then when the time has come to leave this ultra-absorbent haven, you can descend the escalator, don your kagool and return to the rain.

WILL FRANKEN

// BRAVADO //

Bravado, 22 Morningside Road, EH10 4DA. 0131 447 6715, bravadounderwear.co.uk. Mon-Sat 9.30am-5.30pm.

Poppa never got to go to Edinburgh. It just weren't done in his day, a young man going off to fight in Edinburgh. Back then, a fellow stayed where he was and fought. And that's what Poppa did back in America every single day of his life. Poppa fought – everything and everybody. Poppa was a mean man. But funny. Damn funny. If you weren't the one Poppa was being mean at.

With all this talk of Poppa, you out there reading might be thinking I ain't got no Momma. But I do. And Momma never got to go to Edinburgh either.

Momma always told me: "Son, if you should leave the country one day, find yourself a secret place, far away from your wicked Poppa. He's mean to me now—and you find that funny. But soon he'll be mean to you—and I'll find that funny."

Sure enough, one day Poppa was mean to me—and Momma found it funny. So I left home and became a comedian. And, before you know it folks, I was on my way to Edinburgh.

I couldn't fulfil my promise to Momma right away that I'd find a secret place. Let me tell you, come festival time, ain't too many places in Edinburgh that are secret. Everybody all up in your business!

But the last day of the festival, I stumbled upon it! Somewhere near where the A702 meets Morningside Road, there's a lingerie store called Bravado. It's got a nice down-home feel and the girls are mighty helpful. Designer lingerie for modest prices!

And in the dressing room, after shimmying on a red half-slip with matching lace bra, I surveyed my "secret place" and thought of my parents. Thanks, Momma and Daddy, for making me funny!

JANEY GODLEY

// YE OLDE CHRISTMAS SHOPPE //

Ye Olde Christmas Shoppe, 145 Canongate, Royal Mile, EH8 8BN. 0131 557 9220, scottishchristmas.com. Mon-Fri 10am-5.30pm, Sat 10am-6pm, Sun 11am-5pm.

Somewhere in week two of the Edinburgh Fringe, when your soul feels a wee bit tarnished, when you've faced the worst mid-week (we're just going to stare at you) audience, when the Fringe has kicked you in the ovaries just that wee bit too hard, there is an antidote.

There is a place snuggled cheek by jowl to the tartan tat shops on the Canongate where you can find joy and goodwill to all men all year round.

I give you the Ye Olde Christmas Shoppe, which is a firm favourite of Sir Cliff Richard (and he's a clean-living virgin in his nineties, so it must have medicinal properties). You can even look at the photo of Sir Cliff fingering a Santa toy in the window.

Take one step into this red, gold and tinsel covered grotto and you will suddenly feel the worries of bad weather, dodgy ticket sales and incessant brain battering of Oxbridge sketch troupes vanish into the Christmas ether.

Peruse your way through glittery angels and Santa Clauses with sequins and breathe in the seasonal pine; let memories of your Christmas past flood through you as the manmade fibres induce a cluster of hives on your neck. The joy of watching American, Japanese and other world travellers panic buy Christmas goods in August will make you smile and lift your spirits.

Afterwards you can always take your shiny Christmas baubles into your Fringe show and smash them into your own face for the amusement of comedy crowds that hate everything you say but prefer to see you die from a thousand tiny cuts.

The Grassmarket area of Edinburgh is a haven of boutique shops

KATIE GOODMAN

// ORGANIC PLEASURES //

Organic Pleasures is currently relocating - visit organicpleasures.co.uk for updates.

When travelling in a foreign land, after exploring the prerequisite restaurants, finding the right boutique hotel, and reading up on the deadly-boring historical landmarks, what does a modern girl look for? Erotic toy shops, of course.

Especially if you are travelling with only a small carry-on bag and have had the unfortunate experience of being stopped by airport security when the x-ray showed a small unusual object: battery-operated and clearly a weapon of mass destruction. From then on, one would certainly make the smart touristy choice of purchasing such a souvenir from every country she visits. It just makes sense.

Now, this said, I will admit that I wandered into several snazzy stores of this type on my travels several years ago during my Fringe production tour. But I can't remember any details of them, which, if you had to say it, is really a very concise description of a Fringe Festival performer's drunken experience in general.

"Non-toxic booty call, guys? Now, that is gonna get you some action.."

But then there is Organic Pleasures. Now, I have lived in Brooklyn, Malibu, and several other hippie areas and have yet to come across something that touts 'eco-erotic boutique'items such as organic, water-based, dye-free and artificial-color-free lubricants.

I mean, really, have we come a long way, women or what?! Non-toxic booty calls, guys? Now, that is gonna get you some action. Attractive and considerate of our health? You had us at 'sustainably-produced'.

PAUL FOXCROFT

// BLACK LION GAMES //

Black Lion, 90 Buccleuch St, EH8 9NH. 0131 667 2128, black-lion.co.uk. Mon-Sat 10am-6pm.

My first Edinburgh Festival was in 2001. Due to injury, I wasn't able to work for a few days, so a nice local took me to visit Black Lion Games at 90 Buccleuch Street. I spent a quiet, rejuvenating day drinking tea and playing new, unfamiliar board games with the proprietor. I was hooked!

Like a shop from a fantasy novel, it can be hard to find if you are not looking for it (the building is listed, so no signage - just a sandwich board outside), but within it you will find one of the best dedicated games stores in the British Isles, with a mass of games and staff who are happy to help even the swarming masses of the festival as we pollute and sully the great city of Edinburgh with our 'art'.

I have a lot of love for Black Lion Games. In addition to giving me a second home, I bought my first copy of Kill Doctor Lucky there, which then sat in the Bedlam Theatre Cafe for years. In 2006, the delightful Cariad Lloyd and Sara Pascoe picked me up custom cards for Fluxx, the game that we had spent many nights playing in our weird accommodation (they are lovely - go see their shows).

Which leads me to my point: board games are a great resource during the Fringe, a simple escape from all the insanity, insecurity and insincerity of the Fringe; from actually spending that one quiet night in with Settlers of Cataan, to team-building with Pandemic or working out your issues with the betrayal-themed Cosmic Encounter.

Sometimes you need a night off and the guys at Black Lion are there to make yours really fun, so go check them out—or come see one of my shows and I will make some good recommendations.

JIM SMALLMAN

// STUDIO XIII //

Studio XIII Gallery, 3 Jeffrey St, EH1 1DR. 0131 558 2974, stxiii.com.
Mon-Sat 10am-6pm, Sun noon-6pm.

Many comedians, when bored during downtime at the Fringe, may choose to go to a bar and get blind drunk, stay in their flat and play video games, or even go and watch other shows in order to panic about theirs/ feel schadenfreude (delete as appropriate). I, on the other hand, plough all of my pennies and spare moments into getting tattooed.

In 2012 the brilliant Jeff Kohl at Studio XIII inked me with three designs. Two were for publicity purposes, commemorating a wager I made on Twitter and one I made the previous year with fellow stand-up Martin Mor, his bearded face now permanently etched into my shoulder. The third was one I had to symbolise my love for my fiancée as the third week of the Fringe rolled around and I was becoming desperately homesick and daft.

Studio XIII isn't like any other studio. The reception area is a gallery displaying tattoo memorabilia and many of Jeff's designs – if you're a fan of heavy metal or Star Wars (like me) then there are a lot of brilliant, niche designs that are must-sees. Indeed, Jeff isn't like any other artist I have met. A loud, constantly cheerful American, his little tattoo room (dubbed on the sign above the door as 'the torture chamber')

My Secret Edinburgh might not be that much of a secret as most times I am at this place there is always a buzz... literally.

Unbeknownst to a few people, underneath the costume I wear on stage is a selection of tattoos, and most of them have been placed by various tattooists at one of the greatest parlours in the world: Studio 13, just off the Royal Mile and always worth dropping in.

It seem to me as though each year they have a guest artist who manages to capture my feelings of the past month's shows in ink. Some years it can be a simple little something that takes only an hour, but once I spent eight hours in one sitting covering my arm in a selection of pretty things.

Each year I will endeavour to take at least half a day out, normally towards the end to the season, to sit back in a chair and have another reminder placed on my body. Some people find Edinburgh a bit of a sting, but for me, that's what I like. BOY WITH TAPE ON HIS FACE

tells as many stories as he does while he works. He happens to be a huge comedy fan too, having inked many a performer during past Fringes, so he really knows his stuff and will often recommend shows to you whilst making you wince when the needle hits a really tender bit.

Such is my love for this place that I found by accident during August 2012 that I have travelled back several times since to get tattooed by Jeff again (as has my fiancée). It's just as relaxing and friendly as tattoo studios get, provided you like the smell of antibacterial soap, Vaseline, ink and blood and the sound of buzzing needles.

JOEY PAGE

// ARMSTRONG AND SONS //

W Armstrong and Sons, 64-66 Clerk St, EH8 9JB. 0131 667 3056. Also 83 The Grassmarket, EH1 2HJ. 0131 220 5557; and 14 Teviot Place, EH1 2QZ. 0131 226 4634. Al shops Mon-Thu 10am-5.30pm, Fri & Sat 10am-6pm, Sun midday-6pm.

Places like Armstrong and Sons are a perfect way to change the pace if you suddenly feel overgorged on shows. They are probably the only shops in the world where you can stroll in looking for a timeless bit of exuberant clobber and walk out with a vintage board game such as Don't Cook Your Goose (it exists, Google it) or a pot of slime from the film Ghostbusters with Bill Murray's face on the front.

I mean, where better to source a top hat and cape, the purchase of which gives you licence to skulk through the many back alleys just a few hundred metres behind a ghost walk party whilst wearing the combo, rattling a chain and making groaning noises? (The noise is partly in an attempt to spook tourists, and partly because the unrelenting torrential summer rain has soaked through the hole in your shoes.)

Another option is to try your hand in one of Nicholson Street's many wondrous charity shops trying to sell you such delights as a collection of John Candy films on VHS, provided you don't mind chats with middle-aged women about their pet lizards.

Alternatively, nip in for a fur ruff and brown t-shirt that ties at the neck, like Man Utd's green and yellow away strip circa 1992. Get to the top of Arthur's Seat dressed like some sort of pre-historic bearded warrior and claim you are the ruler of all before you, or as I like to do, pop by and get a vintage suit from the 1960s and give the poor local—whose fair city we have invaded—a sitting duck to hurl their abuse, nay, friendly banter at.

Last year a man tried to call me Pete Doherty, but instead shouted: "Oi, Paul Doherty."

PAUL F TAYLOR
// CINEWORLD //

Cineworld Edinburgh, 130/3 Dundee St, EH11 1AF. 0871 200 2000, cineworld.co.uk.

Sometimes the festival can become a bit too much and I want to sit in a dark, air-conditioned room for a few hours. That's why I frequently trek out to the Cinema at Fountain Park.

It is not really a secret because I have seen other people there. But for me it is a really good place to get away from the madness of the festival for a few hours and eat my bodyweight in popcorn.

I first went there when there was a film festival running concurrently to the Fringe and lots of people were queuing up to see these very serious sounding films taking part in the film festival.

I marched straight to the counter and bought a ticket to Transformers. The cashier seemed perplexed that someone would snub these films with artistic integrity for Transformers. He seemed even more perplexed by the Transformer noises I made when I opened my wallet.

UP & OVER IT

// POUNDSTRETCHER //

100-106 South Bridge, EH1 1HN. 0131 225 8540, poundstretcher.co.uk.
Mon-Sat 9am-5pm, Sun 10am-4pm.

Our secret place in Edinburgh is a one-stop shop for performers, techies, visitors, marketeers, aunts and uncles. It is a treasure trove of bargain basement delights, practicality and inspirational randomness. It out-stocks Habitat, Ikea, WH Smith, even Woolworths back in the day. It's Poundstretcher on South Bridge.

You can pretty much buy any prop you could possibly imagine in there. Plastic red onions? Check. Inflatable dolphin? Check. Gold-framed hologram of St Bernadette? Check.

You can buy any size of battery, any colour of electric or gaffer tape, and they even sell projectors! Their cheap candles, bed linen, pans and throws can lighten up the dreariest of digs, and they sell Red Bull by the crate for the terminally hungover.

When given the choice of whether to climb the Scott Monument or spend the afternoon in Poundstretcher, visiting parents always went for Poundstretcher, although they admittedly are from South Wales, so it wasn't a fair contest. They did, however, walk away with Tupperware sandwich boxes for the train journey home, an ornament of a boy weeing for nan, and 24 AA alkaline batteries. All for under a tenner.

Poundstretcher might not be the most glamorous destination but spend enough time with her and she could become your best friend during the Fringe. She's there when you need her most, offering you things you didn't even know existed, never mind wanted. She's a friend, she's a pal, she's Poundstretcher on South Bridge.

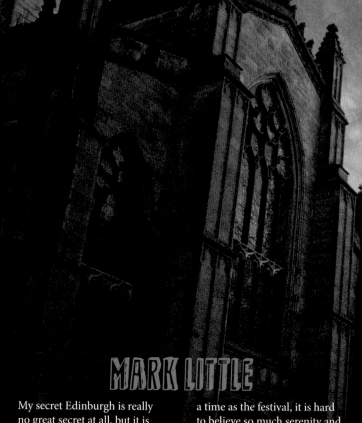

MARK LITTLE

My secret Edinburgh is really no great secret at all, but it is surprising how private and unexplored it can be. It's a place of great beauty and immense solitude, right in the heart of the metropolis. It is a fantastical place as though one has been given the key to enjoy the whole city to oneself. In such a city as Edinburgh, at such a time as the festival, it is hard to believe so much serenity and peace can be enjoyed. The cobbles, castle, gardens and crisp Scottish air combine to create a vast poem to be savoured and read with a uncynical heart. Where and what is this magical place and why would I be fool enough to divulge such a secret? Because, from experience,

I know there is plenty of room for a few more at this most poetical of events. And it is certainly not my secret to keep. Can you tell what it is yet? My secret Edinburgh…is… DAWN!

GYLES BRANDRETH

// STATUE IN PICARDY PLACE //

The first real book I ever read was The Adventures of Sherlock Holmes. Fifty-five years on, I think it is still my favourite book. I was brought up in London. My parents lived in a block of flats above Baker Street Underground station. Out of our kitchen window we could see 221b Baker Street – perhaps the best-known fictional address in the history of literature.

When I first came to Edinburgh to appear in a show on the Fringe, I found a flat right by Picardy Place, where Arthur Conan Doyle, creator of Sherlock Holmes, was born. And a stone's throw from my flat was a larger than life-size bronze statue of my life-long hero, Sherlock Holmes, the world's foremost consulting detective.

The statue was created by Gerald Ogilvie Laing and put on display in Picardy Place in 1989. When I came to the Fringe—first in a show called Zipp!, where we performed one hundred musicals in one hundred minutes, and next in a musical version of Shakespeare's Twelfth Night— part of my daily routine was to visit the statue on my way to the theatre. Every day, to bring me luck, I would touch the great detective's left foot.

© Terry Moran

I suppose I hoped that a smidgeon of his genius might rub off on me.

And then, three years ago, I arrived in Edinburgh for my stand-up debut in the Pleasance Courtyard and, to my considerable alarm, I found that Holmes had gone missing. It wasn't Moriarty, the Napoleon of Crime, who had got the better of him. It was the tram works. My show didn't go too badly, but my month in Edinburgh wasn't quite the same. Something was missing.

And now, happily, that something is back. Edinburgh is rich in remarkable statues—ranging from the mighty monument to Sir Walter Scott on Princes Street to the wee effigy of Greyfriars Bobby, the heroic Skye terrier, on Candlemaker Row—but, for me, none can rival Sherlock Holmes in Picardy Place. He is back where he belongs, close by where his great creator was born in 1859.

My new show at the Pleasance is called Looking for Happiness and, for me, two of the places where I know I can always find it are in the pages of Conan Doyle and by my favourite statue in Picardy Place.

FLANGE KRAMMER

// GOLD POST BOX //

Olympic fever has finally taken hold in Edinburgh. With Sochi 2014 just around the corner, I was excited last year to discover that the post box next to the flat I am staying in during the Edinburgh Festival has been painted gold in my honour.

Some might say that they have been a bit hasty, but I am definitely going to clean up in Russia next year, so why not stay ahead of the game?

Someone tried to tell me it was something to do with the bloke from the Bran Flakes advert, but I correctly dismissed this as British humour.

Some people have said that I could never recreate my skiing success in the world of comedy, but here I am in Edinburgh and, just like on the slopes, I'm going downhill fast.

I had been looking forward to skiing down Arthur's Seat; however, I've been informed that the snow doesn't normally arrive until around mid-September.

DAVID ELMS

// ART //
7 Rutland Ct Ln, EH3 8ES.

My contribution is actually some art, guys, real art. A big bloody bit of stone. Shaped! So if you start to get sick of art that moves around and talks at you, head to between the Sheraton Hotel and Shandwick Place, by the south-west corner of Rutland Square.

I used to go to Edinburgh University and had a flat on Shandwick Place in my final year, and I would walk past this statue pretty much every day. I don't want to give too much away in case any of you do actually see it, but it always did what great art should. It made me question...

1) What the hell is this? I mean really in all my life... what's going on?

2) Who made this? (You'll probably end up assuming it's corporate art, like I did; it's in the middle of office blocks. In that case, what was the brief?)

3) What the hell does it all mean? (This one really had my brain going, to the point where I only just got a 2:1. If any of you do ever see it, let's have a macchiato and jam about this particular Q.)

4) Why is he naked? (I think this about a lot of art). Why does he look so calm?

5) Do horses' legs bend that way?

JAY FOREMA[N]
No Mor[e]
Colour[s]

Pleasance Courty[ard]
8.4[5]

31 July-26 Aug, no[t ...]

'Sharp and sophistic[ated]
classy and funny...Vic[toria]
Wood for the S[...]
generation' Ch[...]

Chris Dangerfield
How I spent £150,000
on Chinese prostitute[s]
in 18 months.

"A natural, physical comedian, a rubber-
physiognomist with superb timing, and
someone who is prepared to hot-wire hi[s]
own psyche in pursuit of emotional rang[e]
Will Se[...]

The Bunka @ The Hive, 6.30pm, 5 - 24 Augus[t]

ANDREW MAXWELL

// THE WATERS OF LEITH //

The actual river for Edinburgh is called the Waters of Leith, and it's a little like a babbling brook over in the north side of the city.

If you approach from the New Town the roads dramatically fall away, if you keep going down those roads you will eventually have to cross a little bridge, which is the river.

Now what I and my aristocratic sidekick Sir Tim do on our days off is head to this river, which is only knee high and flows extremely slowly. What we invented is the sport of dafting, you get two lilos, a cheap bottle of Chilean red wine and you lie on the lilos and float down. You cannot drown, it's ridiculous fun

That's what we do on our day off. The walk is like a canal path, and it eventually goes all the way up to the airport, and the towpath is beautiful. If you walk along the path, joining it at Stockbridge and keep going, it's completely secluded and beautiful. Eventually you come across a little wooden sign which points to the National Scottish Gallery of Modern Art. Go in there, have a look at some art, have a cup of tea, park up your lilo and check out the art.

TONY LAW

// ROYAL BOTANIC GARDENS //

Royal Botanic Garden Edinburgh, Inverleith Row, EH3 5LR. 0131 248 2909, rbge.org.uk. Summer hours daily 10am-5pm.

My favourite spot is in the Botanical Gardens besides the Giant Rhubarb. "I'm a tiny man from the dawn of humanity!! The horror of it all. Where are we going?"

TOMMY HOLGATE
// AMNESTY FOOTBALL MATCH //

Let me tell you something about football. It's a beautiful game. Riddled with unison. British versus German soldiers on Christmas Day? Absolutely.

And the annual Amnesty International Critics vs Comedians game in Edinburgh is in absolutely no way whatsoever dissimilar. Frontliners from both sides of the comedy/performance fence begin lapping each other up like waves approaching one another from juxtaposing ends of the comedy pool. Crashing against each other in a dancing duel of gentlemanly sporting endeavour.

The event is growing year-on-year and in 2012 there were several hundred spectators lining the pitch, with commentary on the microphone from the comedy team's substitute bench.

Mark Watson plays the role of captain to a group of players including Tim Key, Daniel Sloss, Humphrey Ker, Carl Donnelly, Jimeoin, Terry Alderton (former Southend goalkeeper) while the critics team regularly includes Time Out's Editor-in-Chief Tim Arthur, The Independent's Julian Hall and The Guardian's Brian Logan.

Although when I request they pass me the ball, I make sure to shout 'mate' instead of their full name, in case I give away the identity of their face—which would allow any one-star reviewed comedians to pinpoint the impact position of their next tackle.

What was I saying about unison?

Anyway, I have the pleasure of being on both sides of the fence. For the previous two years, as Sun Comedy Columnist, I played for the critics team. This year, though, having severed my tabloid ties to return to my first love, performing, who knows who I'll play for?

Truth be told, I shall still play for the critics out of loyalty (and to avenge last year's 4–3 beating) and proving—once and for all—that it IS possible for us all to get along.

Finally.

For, as Matthew McConaughey once said in a cameo in Sex And The City: "We are animals. Man, woman, walking the Earth, made of head, heart and loins. We're talking about using 'em. Am I right?"

Yes, Matthew, you are always right.

The 2013 Amnesty International charity football match takes place in the Meadows on Sunday August 11, at 3pm

95

FRINGE

BY
PAUL
FOXCROFT

A performer claims not to read reviews, but manages to quote them in the same conversation	Students in white face paint (remember white face paint = legitimate theatre)	Quirky slippering attempt backfires
Respiratory complaint contracted from underground venue	"SATIRE"	You're pretty sure these review quotes are from the 1980s
Nudity on the Royal Mile: Partial - 1pt Full - 2pt Horrific - 5pt	The other kind of anachronistic Shakespeare adaptation	Two people have a conversation where both pretend to remember the other
Hook up! (and then regret)	Walk of Shame 1pt. witnessed 2pt. Experienced 3pt Retroactively deduct.	C Venues does something [] disappoint[] you

HOW IT WORKS

Simply attend the Edinburgh Fringe Festival and either experience or witness the following classic fringe events, sights and grotesque cliches. Then cross them off and tweet

BINGO

Local resident expresses distain	Street theatre mistaken for homeless ... or vice versa	"Oh my god! You've never been up Arthurs seat"
"Yeah, everyones having a bad year..."	Anachronistic Shakespeare adaptation that works	Selective quoting of a terrible review on a flyer "[not] The best show" "[not] Stars!"
OPSTICK!	You buy berocca (it does nothing)	Obvious spelling error in pormotional material
omeone you ow resumes use of Smoking Drinking Class A's	"-but it reads like a four."	Comedian picks on an audience member who is funnier than they are

them at me at @misterspidergod
nd the good folks from Such

Small Portions @smallportions!

RACHEL PARRIS

The Commission

A musical comedy show

.st - 25th August (not 13th)
The Counting House
West Nicholson Street

Free   4pm

"Venomously witty" *Evening Standard*
"Tim Minchin in a frock" *The Londonist*
"mpossibly, infuriatingly good" *Huffington Post*
"Like A Glee Club chick gone wrong" *The Stage*

JONNY
& THE
BAPTISTS
BIGGER THAN JUDAS

'Musical comedy's
rising stars'
Sunday Times

.40PM PLEASANCE DOME

23
PLEASAN
DOME

ELIS JAMES

// SCOTTISH NATIONAL GALLERY //

Scottish National Galery; The Mound, Edinburgh EH2 2EL; 0131 624 6200
Hours: Mon - Sun 10:00 - 17:00 (except Thursday 19:00): nationalgalleries.org

I love the Scottish National Gallery: if anything can make you feel insignificant, it is walking round there for an hour. Some of those paintings are utterly breathtaking, and really put some weirdo saying nasty things about your show on Twitter into perspective.

It was comedian Lloyd Langford who suggested I go last year—he very calmly said 'just go' when I was with him in a pub and it was the best thing I did all Summer.

I'm not usually one for art galleries—I don't really have the patience—but it was spectacular and will definitely be a thing I do every festival.

ADAM HESS

It's not very cool, but my favourite hangout is probably Princes Street Gardens. It is one of the few places that isn't annoyingly overcrowded during the Fringe, and is a great place to get away from all the noise and have a lovely sandwich or cry.

The first time I went to Princes Street Gardens was last year and completely by mistake (I think I was drunk). I tend not to like being too close to open spaces of grass because it suggests I'm probably also near a football or someone with a guitar, but the surroundings, the view and the weather resulted in me having the best packed lunch I had ever had.

As a comedian I tend not to leave the house much during the day and going to parks after dark is pretty rubbish so I made the most of soaking up the sun here last year. It is not your typical park in that it doesn't have condoms and poo littered everywhere, or a slide that requires a tetanus jab to look at, but it is still definitely worth a visit.

My memory of parks as a child isn't great because I used to be scared of ducks and the other children made fun of my bike because it used to be my sister's. If these are the sorts of things that worry you too, then DO NOT WORRY! Everyone here is very friendly and I don't remember any blood-thirsty ducks. People don't bother flyering here and it is too relaxing for anybody to try and be funny, so it's a great place to get away from it all and still be in the heart of the city.

It's also the sort of place where attractive couples lie down in the sun and somehow read the same book together while her head is resting on his chest. So if you are a boyfriend, or indeed a girlfriend, this sickeningly display of happiness could be something you choose to do here. Just make sure you don't stare too much at the drunk comedian guy crying over his packed lunch.

© Chakchouka

100

BEN TARGET

If you seek success when climbing buildings at night, it is advisable to be a) not drunk, and b) a cretin. The views from a summit however are often worth the risk of death by irresponsibility.

On the top floor of a certain academic department in one of Edinburgh's universities is a cistern. It belongs to a toilet. Using the two in conjunction with each other as a sort of stepladder, a ceiling tile can be lifted revealing an attic crawl space. Once inside,

avoid inhaling the insulation fibres and work your way towards the roof hatch. This can be removed with a Phillips screwdriver bought earlier at Pound Savers.

Awaiting the visitor is one of the city's more breathtaking viewing perches. Nestled between Nicolson Street and George IV Bridge, the roof itself is wide enough to play badminton on but doing so would result in a seven-storey plummet. This is a place ambition can be ignored, a place you can enjoy a cup of Bachelor's Oxtail soup.

Future Night Climbers, commit to the rule: respect whatever you touch. Taking care doesn't necessarily reward safe passage but should you accidentally defenestrate yourself, at least it can happen in the knowledge that a double World Heritage site remains intact.

KATIE WILKINS

// THE REAL MARY KING'S CLOSE //

The Real Mary King's Close, 2 Warriston's Close, High St, EH1 1PG. 0845 070 62• realmarykingsclose.com. Festival hours daily 9am-11pm.

Like "The Chicken Man" in Breaking Bad, this place is not so much a secret, as hiding in plain sight. Though unlike Gus Fring, it does not lead a double life as a drugs baron. I assume.

I'm talking of course about the tour at The Real Mary King's Close, just off of the Royal Mile, where you can go down into the tunnels that still run underneath Edinburgh and see where the ghosts of the past walked. I say 'see'; it's actually very dark down there. But very worth doing.

When I went, we had a tour guide dressed in medieval clothing who announced he knew 'nothing of our times' before then asking us to turn off our mobile phones. He also warned us that the ghosts would object to having their photographs taken. It's not everyday you get to come into contact with ghosts, let alone ones that have such a keen understanding of their legal rights. The living could learn a lot from them.

The tour itself is fascinating and makes you forget you are in the middle of a hectic, international festival, with desperate flyerers vying for your attention at every turn. There is something weirdly calming about walking through these cool, dark passageways, retracing the steps of our forebears. And even though you are learning about how devastating and horrific the plague was to the people who once lived here, it does make you put your struggles to get an audience for your show into perspective.

It is definitely worth doing if you want to be taken out of yourself and transported out of the festival to a simpler and more brutal time for a little while, and share in some of Edinburgh's rich history.

FOOD

POSH NOSH

Posh Nosh

FOOD

LLOYD GRIFFITH
// MOTHER INDIA //

Mother India, 3-5 Infirmary St, EH1 1LT, 0131 524 9801, motherindia.co.uk. Mon-Thu midday-2pm, 5pm-10.30pm, Fri & Sat midday-11pm, Sun midday-10pm.

Whenever I go to Edinburgh for the festival I always make sure I visit Mother India at least once a week. Whenever I have friends or family up, that's the first place I take them. If you have never been then you are missing out.

It is an absolutely gorgeous Indian restaurant but with a twist, and that twist is tapas. Basically, you have your signature Indian dishes but in smaller portions, just like tapas. Genius.

I heartily recommend the sag paneer, lamb karahi and the chilli king prawns. They recommend that you get two to three dishes each, and it's a great idea as you can then share with your party. The food tastes amazing and the one thing that everyone that I have taken has noticed is that there is never any grease on the plates when you have finished. Always a bonus.

Mother India is a very popular haunt, so make sure you get there early or try and book.

Posh Nosh

FOOD

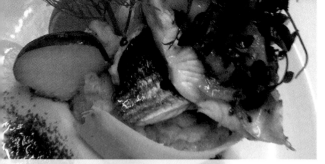

ALISTAIR BARRIE
// SWEET MELINDA'S //

Sweet Melindas, 11 Roseneath St, EH9 1JH. 0131 229 7953, sweetmelindas.co.uk. Mon-Sat noon-2pm and Tues-Sat 6-10pm.

© Sweet Melindas

Posh Nosh

FOOD

Every time I play the festival I stay in Marchmont as it is close to everything, but that little stretch of Meadow means you feel separated from the madness. It is also perfect to walk/dance/cry/sing/laugh/stagger across at any time of day or night.

Marchmont is also home to Sweet Melinda's, which I discovered thanks to a chance recommendation in 2004. It's not a secret at all, but it is everything a neighbourhood restaurant should be. They are next door to the brilliant Eddie's Seafood Market, which the chef visits every morning, and the food and service are superb.

I have eaten there with friends, colleagues, my parents and Rolf Harris, and have already booked a table this year for the team behind No Pressure To Be Funny, as we are all massive champagne socialists who require fine dining in order to turn in a good show.

As I write a restaurant blog called Food Ponce—see alistairbarrie. com—Sweet Melinda's can expect a write-up which will probably be the sort of review most performers would sell their grandparents for. My grandparents, incidentally, are no longer with us, but remain very much available to the highest bidder.

MARCUS BRIGSTOCKE

© Lisa Clarke

BAR NAPOLI // COMEDY VENUES // ROYAL MILE

Bar Napoli, 75 Hanover St, EH2 1EE. 0131 225 2600, barnapoliedinburgh.co.uk.
Sat-Wed noon-2am, Thu & Fri noon-3.30am.

I have several favourite places in Edinburgh.

The first is Bar Napoli on Hanover Street; it has a menu with over 700,000 dishes on it and the three I have tasted are delicious. The atmosphere is wonderful; it's full of festival folk and the seafood is to die for.

One my favourite places at the festival is sitting in the warm darkness at the back of a small venue watching a fellow comedian's show, seeing them spin laughter and joy out of the air, delighting in their talent and wit and the roar of audience approval.

One of my other favourite places at the festival is sitting in the stifling darkness of a small venue, watching a fellow comedian's

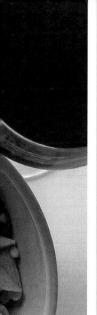

BRENDON BURNS

After hours I prefer a sit down meal to going out drinking. Bar Napoli is my favourite late night eatery.

It is run by loud Scottish Italians and has a huge menu. Plus they always give me a discount, so go in and try saying you're me and see what happens.

Whatever you do, don't goose the waiters like my friend Rob once did though. They made it quite clear that if he weren't with me he would have been stabbed.

how and seeing them die on their arse, delighting in their self-delusion and failure to win the audience round and create anything more than a despairing sigh from the reviewer on the second row.

The top of Arthur's Seat is a must and excellent for clearing thoughts of the festival beneath you from your mind.

The centre of the Royal Mile—if you complain about the participants of the biggest and best arts festival in the entire world shoving their flyers in your hands whilst dressed as Helen of Troy but in sunglasses trying to promote 'To Helen Back!!!' you've missed the point of the festival.

We're lucky to have it. I love it. Embrace it and see as much stuff as your wallet allows.

ALEXIS DUBUS
// CHEZ JULES //

109 Hanover St, EH1 4DJ. 0131 226 6992, chezjulesbistro.com. Sun-Thu noon-midnight, Fri & Sat noon-midnight.

This little eatery lies just off Edinburgh's George Street. And, yes,
quelle surprise, I've opted for a French restaurant. But enculez-vous,
I've chosen Chez Jules as my little Edinburgh "point chaud" (hot
spot) for a reason. There are plenty of excellent French restaurants
to choose from in Edinburgh, should you wish to present a surprise
waft of garlic to the collective faces of your already sweltering
audience that night, but this establishment holds a special place in
my heart ever since a visit there on Bastille Day 2011, while in the
city to perform at the equally excellent, if mildly less garlicky Stand
Comedy Club round the corner.

Cyrano de Bergerac's nose was the first thing to greet me as I was
led to my 'table pour un', the D'Artagnans and Marie Antoinettes
hurriedly receiving and ferrying orders to and fro, the most

© Chez Jules

There is a French restaurant called Chez Jules on Hanover Street which never seems to close and always seems to be full of comics.

I once ordered a dish that roughly translated as 'simple chicken', and everybody laughed at me for being very small town and unadventurous. So the next time I ordered snails, frogs legs and anything else that sounded like food from a Roald Dahl book.

The food's excellent though, and as long as you don't go with eight comedians who will take the piss out of everything, you can order whatever you want.

ELIS JAMES

enjoyable part being that some staff were far less into it than others. I would love to have heard the Gallic sighs at the meeting as Monsieur Jules (was he de Bergerac that night?) put forward his plans for the evening of 'La Grande Fête'.

So I got to enjoy a delicious pre-gig meal combining two of my favourite things: onion soup and awkwardness. I have been back several times since to that cosy, rustic hideaway and have thoroughly enjoyed it every time, but I would highly recommend getting down there on 14 July to maximise the Frenchness of your experience. Bon appétit.

ZOE LYONS

© The Witchery

// THE WITCHERY //

Castlehill, Royal Mile, EH1 2NF. 0131 225 5613, thewitchery.com. Daily 5.30-11.30pm, Sat & Sun midday-3pm.

I survive most things in life by thinking about my next meal. I am as food-focused as a hungry terrier; it pretty much forms the entire framework of my day. Everything else has to slot around my nibble schedule. Just to prove the point my show this year is at 5pm, a time chosen because I figured out that factoring in post-show adrenaline rush my digestive system will be ready for dinner about 7.30pm, which is perfect.

The timings might be right but often the nosh isn't quite so peachy. Anyone who has ever done a month at the Edinburgh Festival will tell you it is often the closest they come to succumbing to scurvy or rickets. Fruit and veg can easily become the stuff of legends as chips with sauce find themselves becoming a stable of most performers' diets.

I can live like that as long as I know there is light at the end of the tunnel, and my culinary illumination comes in the form of a trip to the Witchery Restaurant. It is my Edinburgh guilty pleasure. It is a beautiful fine dining restaurant at the top of the Royal Mile, practically underneath the castle. It is so beautiful at night with candles on the steps as you descend into the Secret Garden dining room. It also looks a bit like it has been built as the set of a Dracula movie, with candelabras, drapes, and goblet glasses.

I bloody love it. I go with my other half on the last day of the Fringe and have a massive gastronomic blowout. After a month of avoiding reviews, avoiding rain and, let's be honest, avoiding some people, it is my time to dive in and enjoy. A delicious slice of decadence to end the month, it means I always leave the Edinburgh Fringe with a splendid taste in my mouth, and how many comics can say that?

PAUL ZERDIN
// THE WITCHERY //

I like eating out, and in Edinburgh the Witchery is my favourite place. It is fantastic, right up under the castle, visiting it is just like going back in the time. It's tucked away so if you don't know about it you wouldn't find it, but enter through the tunnel and into the restaurant and it's like entering another century.

There is a mystical garden space and a really nice main chamber that is steeped in history. I love all of it. I just want to be in there somewhere: I don't care where.

I went for my first Edinburgh in 1999, taken there by my ex-wife for my birthday. I fell in love with it and decided: I am just going to keep coming back here. I have since taken friends, and had joint birthdays there. It is a good night out: there is a great ambience, especially if you have got family up and you want somewhere to go after a show.

I have never had bad food there; it is European cuisine with some great fish. I am a health freak so it's good there is healthy stuff available, but there's lots of great red wine too. And the staff know it is a special night for you, so they really help give the feel that you are somewhere exclusive.

Last year there was one night where I tried to take my parents there but we couldn't get in, so we went to their sister restaurant. It was nice, but it didn't quite have the magic of the Witchery. My girlfriend has never been so I'll be taking her this year.

The Witchery is nice for special occasions, but I also like Howie's. It is a great place to go for lunch or a bite to eat – they do haggis spring rolls that are just sublime. You can have a couple of those as a main and a bottle of red before starting an evening's drinking.

KATIE MULGREW

// MAMMA'S //

30 The Grassmarket, EH1 2JU. 0131 225 6464, mammas.co.uk. Sun-Thu midday-11pm, Fri & Sat midday-midnight.

The very first time I came to Edinburgh was because of a boy.

I had just started doing stand up and just started courting (yes, courting, we need fancy verbs for such a fancy city) said boy when he had to depart to work at the Edinburgh Fringe for a month.

I decided I would surprise him with a visit. An eight-hour bus journey later with probably the worst hangover I've ever had and I had arrived. I walked around Edinburgh in awe. The buildings, the atmosphere, I felt like Dorothy in the Emerald City. Only after a lot more Jagerbombs.

Unfortunately my plan was ruined by my own inability to navigate Edinburgh's cobbled roads and steep hills without a smartphone app.

"HELLOI'MINEDINBURGHIDON'TKNOWWHEREANYTHINGIS-IT'S'SBLOODYMASSIVEANDANDMYNOKIAISDYING. SURPRISE!"

The boy found me—well a sweaty, disheveled version of my former self—outside the Café Royale. Like the start of all great romances he took me promptly to a shower and then promptly for food at Mama's on the Grassmarket.

We shared a pizza, his half-laden with jalapenos, my half with olives. I remember it being the best pizza I've ever had, but possibly because it was the best date I've ever had.

He supped beer and I supped vodka with Diet Coke and we chatted away until the wax candle on our table had melted clean down. Until the surrounding tables were all stacked with chairs and until our waitress began giving us 'oh, do fuck off' eyes. I spent the rest of my trip negotiating Edinburgh's cobbled roads and steep hills with him.

That weekend I fell madly in love with that city and madly in love with that boy. Marrying him next year.

NADIA KAMIL

// TOWER RESTAURANT - MUSEUM OF SCOTLAND //

@ Tower Restaurant

The Tower, National Museum of Scotland, Chambers St, EH1 1JF. 0131 225 3003, tower-restaurant.com. Daily 10am-11pm.

Having a birthday in August means growing up without ever having your school friends pay any attention to it. Maybe that is why I have spent nearly every August since leaving school at the Edinburgh festival.

My 20th was probably my best ever birthday. I was playing Tinkerbell in a university production of Peter Pan. The cast and crew spent the whole day paying attention to me, which I loved. Eventually they got me very drunk in a restaurant where I had a belly-off against the resident belly dancer. The next day, Tinkerbell came very close to spewing in the Lost Boy's hideout.

The following year was an awkward dinner with the sketch group I was in (and not really getting on with) plus my dad. We accidentally went to a gay restaurant near Broughton Street.

My dad generously offered to pay for everyone as a treat for my birthday and I thought they were pricks for accepting because him paying for anything for them was in no way a treat for me. If anything, it was less birthday money directly in cash for me.

I am still not over this. In 2010 I visited the festival around my birthday. My boyfriend was doing a show and I came up to reassure him it was good enough to keep me interested and was funny, clever etc. In return for this service I naively expected him to arrange something nice for my birthday.

When it transpired he had planned literally nothing (literally nothing), I harrumphed us out of the flat and demanded he take me somewhere nice. He failed to make any decisions and we walked (I stomped) around town until I spotted an offer for afternoon tea in the National Museum of Scotland. The Tower Restaurant at the top of the Museum of Scotland is quite posh and a bit expensive but the views are mega. You can walk up to a sort of turret/platform which gives you spectacular views across the whole of Edinburgh. The effect is quite calming if you're stressing out because your boyfriend is a bit useless or your show is not selling or you think you're not getting the buzz you deserve.

Seeing the sea, the castle, the dramatic Scottish skies, the small people below scuttling about the festival, can make you realise how small and pointless your worries are. And the afternoon tea is really nice.

NISH KUMAR

// KAMPONG AH LEE //

28 Clerk St, EH8 9HX. 0131 662 9050, kampongahlee.co.uk.
Mon-Thu noon-3pm, 5-11pm. Fri-Sun noon-11pm.

This is a real gem of a restaurant, easily one of my favourites in Edinburgh, in spite of its low-key appearance and the second half of its name, which sounds like a botched attempt to Google Translate a south-east Asian sexual position.

What this lacks in elaborate decor, it makes up for in excellent Malaysian food. The Laksa has reinvigorated me after many an exhausting day of shows and, crucially for anyone at the Fringe, it is eminently affordable.

One year I took my cousin, a resident of the city of Edinburgh. In a burst of teenage arrogance, he demanded the waiter bring him 'the hottest dish on the menu'.

The resulting chili lamb was less a serving of food, and more a piece of culinary ballistics.

We were both instantly in tears; my cousin weeping with pain and me crying tears of laughter at his self-inflicted pain. So not only did I have a fantastic meal, but we also learned a valuable lesson about food-based hubris.

CARIAD LLOYD
// SPOON //

6a Nicolson St, EH8 9DH. 0131 623 1752, spoonedinburgh.co.uk.
Mon-Sat 10am-11pm, Sun midday-5pm.

© Spoon

There is a doorway on Nicolson Street that at a quick 'I'm late for a show, why is the Pleasance Dome not nearer' glance might look like an entrance to a sofa showroom.

The glass doors lead on to a pretty wooden staircase, and you will see tourists peering in, unsure of what is waiting for them at the top, a gaggle of kagools guessing at the bottom.

If you are new to Edinburgh, and indeed the festival, you will march past it; you are late, after all. But after a few festivals, the idea of somewhere you can just sit becomes a mythical place to think of late at night. Just somewhere to have a sit down. Without a flyer or a poster in view. Just a lovely sit down.

And when finally the idea of somewhere peaceful becomes more precious than keeping the ring from Boromir, and that glass door becomes more inviting than someone offering to do your tech for free, you head upstairs and you find Spoon, a huge, airy, friendly bistro filled with Edinburgh locals, their faces unsullied by flyer ink and self-hatred.

The tables are roomy, the tea comes in china cups and the food is good. And they let you sit there; they don't kick you out. You can stay there and Google your own name and weep in peace, or quietly read your brilliant reviews. And sit. Breathe. And finally, sit.

SHAZIA MIRZA

// PECKHAM'S //

49 South Clerk St, EH8 9NZ. 0131 668 3737, peckhams.co.uk. Mon-Sat 8am-10pm, Sun 9am-10pm.

This is a place where I go to stick my face in some really posh food. Edinburgh is so stressful that nice, good, expensive food brings huge comfort.

I would never eat this food in real life, and I certainly wouldn't eat it every day as it is far too expensive. But the Edinburgh Festival is not real life, and what's expensive when you have spent a million pounds to put a show on? I do love this shop. I hide here for hours, and it is great because it is open really late.

When I have had a bad gig I go there, get a huge basket and fill it with cream cakes, full fat cheeses, smoked salmon pizette, baked brie in phyllo with mango chutney and other foods, the names of which I can't pronounce. It makes me feel better just filling up that basket.

Then I go home and stuff my face with all the food in one sitting. The fancy names of the foods make me feel rich and I automatically feel better. When my face is full of caviar truffles, dying on stage, debt and misery have no feeling at all. All negativity evaporates into the ether and all I can smell is Blacks' organic green and orange tea.

There are many branches of Peckham's, but my favourite is on South Clerk Street in Edinburgh. I love that it is not in the city centre. The last thing I want is to see other comedians watching me wallow in the misery of a raspberry blancmange. I can walk round quietly in disguise, spend hours reading the labels on the food – also therapeutic – and then spend more time picking things up, putting them in my basket and then putting them back on the shelf.

I go there every day when I am at the Edinburgh Festival. It's the ultimate escapism.

Posh Nosh

FOOD

JOHN LUKE ROBERTS

// SUSHIYA //

19 Dairy Road, EH11 2BQ. 0131 313 3222, sushiya.co.uk.
Tue-Sun noon-2.30pm and Tue-Thu & Sun 5-10.30pm, Fri & Sat 5-11pm.

Hey guys, I've been to Japan. Yep. I'm the kind of man who goes to Japan. Yep. I'm also the kind of man who tells you about it. Yep. The two weeks I spent there were a whirlwind of relaxation and fun*. In other words, pretty much the opposite of the Edinburgh Fringe, which is four tortuous weeks of wildly fluctuating levels of self-esteem and suffocating desperation. That's not hops you smell when you get off the train into Edinburgh Waverley; it's the frenzied anxiety of thousands of performers. And hops as well, actually. You were, to an extent, right about the hops.

If you would like to escape the Edinburgh Fringe and pretend you are in Japan, why not go to Sushiya, near Haymarket station? The food is delicious, reasonably priced, and, unlike in the Japanese-style restaurant opposite the Pleasance Dome, I have never had an international student ask my girlfriend out on a date while I was sitting right next to her in Sushiya.****

*Note I chose the word 'whirlwind' instead of another metaphorical natural disaster, thus resisting having two jokes** in this article for the sake of good taste. But also note that I have alerted you to that fact, in a pathetic attempt to have my cake and eat it. That's also, unfortunately, the type of man I am.***

** Yes! There's another joke later on!

*** I already feel bad about this and am leaving these footnotes in purely in the name of deservedly shaming myself rather than attempting to earn some kind of perverse respect. I had a lovely time there. Everyone was so polite.

**** As you now know, I lied about there being another joke later on.

CHRIS MARTIN
// MUSSEL AND STEAK BAR //

Mussel and Steak Bar, 110 West Bow, Grassmarket, EH1 2HH. 0131 225 5028, mussel-landsteakbar.com. Mon-Thu noon-2.45pm, 6-10pm, Fri-Sun noon-10pm.

I don't really know what to say about this place that isn't blindingly obvious.

If you hate steak and mussels then you probably shouldn't go here, unless you are trying to be ironic or method acting as someone that likes putting these foods in your belly.

If you like both these foods then go here. I went there with my massive dad last year and he nearly did a food orgasm all over the table.

That disgusting and graphic image aside, it's cracking. Yes, please!

Posh Nosh

FOOD

126

HARDEEP SINGH KOHLI
// ONDINE //

© Ondine

Ondine, 2 George IV Bridge, EH1 1AD. 0131 226 1888, ondinerestaurant.co.uk.
Festival hours daily midday-3pm, 5.30-10pm

Now that I live in Edinburgh I relate to the city in a very different way. Previously I might have sought solitude in Holyrood Park or embraced the earthy appeal of the now regenerated Leith, the prostitutes and down dirty drinking dens a now distant memory. 2013 has me as a denizen of castle city so my escape is perhaps a little less obvious.

They say the best restaurant is the one where you are known. I suppose that why I love Ondine. The chef/proprietor Roy Brett is one of the loveliest men I have ever met and an exceptional chef at that. One of the main reasons I decided not to return to London was the quality of food in Scotland's capital city.

Ondine is one of those places that changes with the day. A bright lunch soon becomes an atmospheric evening and more often than not I will be there at the bar come closing. The food is superb and I work in the kitchen every now and again, if only to remind myself how little I actually know about cooking!

Posh Nosh

FOOD

© David Bann

TRODD EN BRATT
// DAVID BANN //

David Bann, 56-58 St Mary's St, EH1 1SX. 0131 556 5888, davidbann.com. Festival hours Sun-Thu 11am-10pm, Fri & Sat 11am-10.30pm.

If you want to treat yourself in Edinbubble, why not do it the guilt-free, meat-free way by going to David Bann's restaurant on St Mary's Street? That's how we roll! You won't even notice there's no meat in, we promise! It's 'world food', so Aubergine, Chickpea and Cashew Koftas and Chilli Filo Tart with Sweet Potato and Chocolate Sauce are the sorta tuck which adorn the menu - nom NOM NOMMM...

And anyone who has Rhubarb Cake and Vanilla Cream on the menu should be a friend for life, right? This is Edinburgh's finest vegetarian restaurant – we're sure of it. We would advise booking but you can't during the festival, so don't.

On 2011 we had a girls night out there with Pippa Evans and Jules (who was teching for us on The Showstoppers) – it was the perfect atmosphere to celebrate a birthday and be virtuous. It was a million miles away from the bustle of the Royal Mile. You could even dress up a bit and that'd be all right if you like that sort of thing!

EDINBURGH CAN BE SOOO CASUAL. Bratt even ate beetroot and she hates beetroot. Trodd was persuaded to have wine too, it was so relaxing. A veritable sanctuary and we shall be returning this year once we've won Edinburgh.

CATIE WILKINS

// RUAN SIAM //

Ruan Thai, 48 Howe St, EH3 6TH. 0131 226 3675, ruanthai.co.uk. Mon-Sat mid-day-2.30pm, daily 5.30-10.30pm.

There is a Thai restaurant I really like going to, slightly off the beaten track called The Ruan Siam, on Howe Street. The food is really delicious (I am a massive fan of Thai food).

It is also a good place to go to if you want to escape from the madness of the festival for a bit. Because it's slightly out of the way from the centre of the action, it feels much calmer. You don't get flyered on the way in, or bump into 20 people you know and feel obliged to talk to. Nobody makes you do shots and calls you names if you say, 'I can't, my liver hurts.'

Not that I don't like bumping into all the lovely people I know in Edinburgh. It's not like I am massively socially awkward or have a personality disorder or anything. It's definitely not that. I am normal. I just really like Thai food.

JAMIE DEMETRIOU

// LEVEN'S //

Leven's, 30 Leven St, EH3 9LJ. 0131 229 8988. Daily midday-2.30, 5.30-11pm.

Sometimes I even like to eat at a place called Leven's. It serves Thai fusion meals. These guys will fuse literally anything with Thaisian foods. A Thai curry sauce with a British piece of chicken, a glass of Scottish water with a Thai ice. I even once saw them Thai-dye a Welsh egg.

Seriously though, I love this restaurant and the way its food tastes. It's in my Top One of all the restaurants in the city.

CASTLE

QUICK BITES

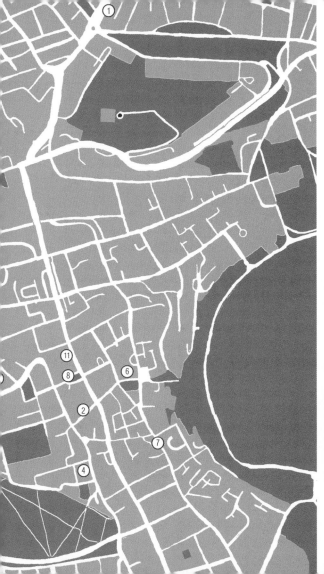

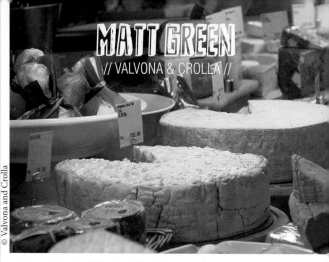

Valvona & Crolla, 19 Elm Row, EH7 4AA. 0131 556 6066, valvonacrolla.co.uk. Mon-Thu 8.30am-5.30pm, Fri & Sat 8am-6pm, Sun 10.30am-3.30pm.

I came to the Fringe for the first time as a student as part of a sketch show, and our flat was pretty much directly opposite Valvona & Crolla. It is an amazing deli and café bar which sold (and still sells) the most amazing breads, meats and cheeses, as well as all sorts of other delicious things that I really couldn't afford. Unfortunately my greed (and laziness) overtook my financial sense and I ended up spending an unwisely large proportion of my student loan in there!

At that time (I'm talking 1998, practically the Olden Days) it was hard to find any decent food in Edinburgh to take away, especially if you weren't keen on chips or deep fried anything, so in my mind Valvona & Crolla became a little oasis of quality cuisine in a sea of Greggs. Since then I have found many other great places to eat, but V&C will always have a special place in my heart.

I pop back in every year for a bit of nostalgia (and Parma ham). I think they also do Fringe shows in the back room, although I've never seen anything there. I'm too busy drooling over the cheeses. To be honest, they're not very keen when I do that.

JACOB EDWARDS
// VALVONA & CROLLA //

A special place to go during the Edinburgh Festival for me has always been Harvey Nichols. Nothing says Scotland to me than a department store founded in London in the 1880s. It's my first port of call when I want to check out what's new in the ever-changing, fast-paced world of Scottish fashion.

Of course, the idea of actually going to Harvey Nichols while the world's largest arts festival goes on around it is moronic. So why have I spent so much time there in past years? Probably because, unlike many of the venues one plays during the festival, Harvey Nichols has the kind of air conditioning that can only be described as luxuriant. Serious game-changing climate control.

Really though, if you are looking for a secret Edinburgh gem, I'd heartily recommend Valvona & Crolla.

This is an astonishing deli, food hall, wine shop & café/restaurant that looks like a bog-standard newsagent from the outside, but is a veritable Aladdin's cave of Italian goodness upon entry—like the Tardis, in that it tastes much better on the inside than it looks from the outside.

Valvona & Crolla remains home to the best coffee I've ever had, even better than Harvey Nichols. No, really.

MAX & IVAN
// MOSQUE KITCHEN //

Mosque Kitchen, 33 Nicolson St, EH8 9BX. 0131 667 4035, mosquekitchen.com. Daily 11.30am-11pm.

When we first visited Edinburgh as dewy-eyed undergraduates, the Mosque Kitchen quite genuinely saved our lives.

For unimaginably small sums of money one could purchase huge portions of real, hearty food: steaming curry, infinite quantities of rice, gloopy, nourishing dahl and succulent kofte kebabs. It was stodgy, it was served up on paper plates and eaten under a tarpaulin in an invariably rainy car park, but it was heaven. It was the only way we survived a month of performing in an atrocious 'edgy' piece of 'new writing' whilst suffering from chronic sleep-deprivation and cirrhosis of the everything.

And then something changed. Gradually, as we returned—in comedy shows of our own devising—the Mosque Kitchen started to get... corporate.

"...the Mosque Kitc[hen] quite genuinely sav[ed] our lives..."

The prices went up, only incrementally, but still. And then, horror of horrors, last year it had moved—from its beloved quasi-legal car park arrangement to an actual *indoor* building, with *real* chairs—not the combination of benches, plastic garden furniture and caked-on pigeon faeces we had come to love and expect.

So what next? As we write this, there is every chance that they will have a 'menu', or that you'll need to 'book', or that a three-course meal will actually cost £10. If that's the case, we will mainly be happy for the success of the hardworking folk who run the Mosque Kitchen, yet we will also mourn the passing of a wonderful era.

But until then, we raise a lukewarm can of Rubicon Mango to the finest cash-only Mosque-run Edinburgh-based canteen we've ever eaten at.

NATHANIEL METCALFE
// MOSQUE KITCHEN //

A couple of years ago I fell in love with the curry that they were serving in the bar of the Pleasance Dome. I would go around telling anyone who would listen how nice it was and bragging that it only cost a fiver.

Everyone must have been laughing behind my back because it turned out the Mosque Kitchen were supplying the Pleasance Dome with the curry, and not only was THIS Mosque Kitchen just around the corner from the Dome, but it was also EVEN cheaper. What a mug I had been.

GARETH MORINAN
// MOSQUE KITCHEN //

I want to recommend the Baklava they sell at the Mosque Kitchen. Forget that savoury curry nonsense that is apparently so popular on this island. No, it's all about that sweet honey/nut/green/pastry type thing they serve as a dessert. It's truly the best Baklava in the world (probably/maybe/I have no evidence to back up that claim).

Also I don't want to overstate the importance of this eatery, but I think it once and for all proves that Islam is a positive force in this world. Whenever I hear people unfairly make claims about how Muslims follow a violent religion, I look them in the eyes and say: "I challenge you to say that again after eating a Baklava from the Mosque Kitchen!"

I invite all would-be Islamaphobes to undertake the Baklava challenge. As of yet I've had no uptake on that offer. (Just to clarify: it is fine to go eat the Baklava, even if you are not an Islamaphobe.)

CHRIS BOYD
// SAIGON SAIGON //

Saigon Saigon, 14 South St, EH2 2AZ. 0131 5573737, saigonrestaurant.co.uk. Daily midday-11pm, lunch buffet midday-4pm.

One of the greatest battles I often face at the Fringe is not piling on loads of weight and becoming very unhealthy through the endless cycle of alcoholic beverages and late-night greasy food intake. Having said that, I am quite partial to an All-You-Can-Eat Chinese buffet as much as the next man who has never visited China.

I often try to make a pilgrimage to Edinburgh's All-You-Can-Eat buffet at least once a week. I can't really remember where it is. I'm usually either very tired or very drunk, like a right bloody bloke, when I go there but it's somewhere central and if you seek it out, like Narnia, the rewards are endless.

It is a little more pricy than the usual AYCE fair—about £10—but the meat tastes like proper meat and for that you also get those prawns that you have to shell yourself. Proper posh. And they don't charge you a service charge, which is good, since you are serving yourself. Do not fill up on rice though. That would be my one word of advice. Another personal favourite place is situated between The Royal Mile and the Pleasance. Opposite that poster of Jimmy Carr that someone graffitied the other year.

It's a passage between two buildings called Boyd's Entry. I usually walk past there and point at the sign and go 'Eh? Funny in't it, that?' to whoever I'm with. We do laugh.

Meadow Bar, 42-44 Buccleuch St, EH8 9LP. 0131 667 6907. Daily midday-1am.

© Meadow Bar

It's not really a secret as it is a Laughing Horse Free Fringe venue, but it is possibly one of my favourite venues. I have done several shows at the Meadow Bar on Buccleugh Street; it's a room above a pub with a toilet right in the middle.

What people might not know about this place is that the food is amazing! As in five-star delicious! As someone who owns a Taste card and has no issues dining out table for one, this place is the best place to eat in Edinburgh!

It has got all your standard meals but all really well-made, fresh and delicious! The chef, Zac, is incredible and if I ever have need for a private chef, he will be it!

Last year they named a burger after me as that's how often I frequent it. It's a veggie burger with cheese and wedges instead if chips, cheese on the wedges and a fried egg instead of salsa. I love meat, but this is the best burgers I have ever eaten! The prices are so reasonable and it is really worth the trek.

The staff are amazing, the food is delicious and the shows are some of the best on the fringe. I absolutely love It, The Meadow bar really is the best place to catch some hidden gems.

MUMS
GREAT COMFORT FOOD

ISY SUTTIE

// MUM'S //

Mum's, 4a Forrest Road, EH1 2QN. 0131 260 9806, monstermashcafe.co.uk. Mon-Sat 9am-10pm, Sun 10am-10pm.

Nestled between The Meadows and Grassmarket is a brilliant place called Mum's, a carnivores' carnival of endless sausage, mash and other comfort foods, with good veggie options too.

I first discovered it at the perilous three-week point in the festival about seven years ago, with approximately six pints of Stella-with-a-vodka-top coursing round my veins.

'Twas a very hungover morning when Danielle Ward decided that only Monster Mash—the old name for Mum's—would silence my cries.

I dragged my limp body through the door and it was like entering a paradise where the angels are made of meat and the clouds of potato, with pies inexplicably floating around. It took my booze-addled brain approximately four minutes to decide which type of sausage to have, then a further two minutes to settle on the mash (black pudding and apple is a particular favourite). And if that's not enough, they do lots of different gravies and school-type desserts.

I think it is the school dinners thing which strikes a chord in me, and since that drizzly morning I've sought out the cafe whenever I need a bit of a boost during the festival. Retro is everywhere now, but while the rather ominous (when you're 34) school disco and Bros/2Unlimited mash-ups languish at the bottom of the pile of what is acceptable, Mum's is firmly atop, evoking memories of dinner ladies in those peach dresses with the squares on them, or the time Joe Jones flicked custard at me and I didn't wipe it off all day.

But above all, the food is great and so is the atmosphere. And not a peach dress in sight.

Quick Bites

FOOD

JOSH WIDDICOMBE

// RED BOX NOODLE BAR //

Red Box Noodle Bar, 51-53 W Nicolson St Edinburgh EH8 9DB
0131 662 0828, Open 12:00-22:00 daily; red-boxnoodlebar.co.uk

The Red Box Noodle Bar makes me excited about Edinburgh from about May.

On a Saturday you will queue out onto the street but it is worth it as it is the most comforting food of a long month. But do be aware it is cash only, a half hour queue for being told that can be the final nail in the coffin.

DOUG SEGAL

// BONSAI BAR BISTRO //

Bonsai Bar Bistro, 46 West Richmond St, EH8 9DZ. 0131 668 3847, bonsaibarbistro.
co.uk. Daily noon-10pm. Also at 14 Broughton St, EH1 3RH. 0131 557 5093. Sun-Thu
12.30-10.30pm, Fri & Sat 12.30-11.30pm.

Edinburgh. Land of the deep fried Mars bar and stovies. A place where it is impossible to get really good, healthy food without paying a fortune, I was told.

Au contraire! (he said with a nod to the auld alliance). There is superb, great value sushi to be had at Bonsai Bar Bistro.

Some of the best and most authentic sushi you will find outside of Tokyo at great prices: Tako salad (marinated octopus and tomato with yuzu dressing) for £3.95; yake hotate (seared scallops with ginger & orange) for £6.95 and eight pieces of soft shelled crab gaijin sushi for £8.95.

It is just around the corner from The Pleasance and wonderfully close to the flat I am renting. It's a really nice place to just chill and have a beer away from all the hustle too.

See you there?

MATT LACEY
// KISMOT //

29 St Leonards St, EH8 9QN. 0131 667 0123, kismot.co.uk. Wed-Mon 4.30-
11.

A few years ago I tried a spoonful of the curry that was brought to fame in articles around the world: "'Killer Kismot curry' contest leaves two in hospital in Edinburgh". It was painful on the way in and painful on the way out, though this probably wouldn't surprise you about a food that is so spicy the diner has to sign a waiver before they eat.

The waiter brings it over to the table in a gas mask, and I wouldn't be surprised if the fumes were a rudimentary tear gas. But if you don't order the killer, the food is pretty nice at the Kismot curry house and it's right next to the Pleasance, so pretty convenient for the festival.

Although, if either alcohol or bravado makes you sample the Kismot Killer, I would recommend putting the toilet roll in the fridge when you get home...

HOWARD READ

// ELEPHANT AND BAGELS //

Elephant and Bagels, 32 Marshall St, EH8 9BJ. 0131 668 4404, elephanthouse.biz. Mon-Fri 8am-10pm, Sat 9am-11pm, Sun 9am-10pm.

One of my favorite places is Elephant and Bagels, just off Nicolson Street. The first two times I performed at the Fringe our flat was opposite what we were pretty sure was a brothel, and a couple of doors down from Elephant And Bagel. I chose the bagels. To eat, that is. The Fringe can be a lonely place when you're far away from the one you love for a month, but it is a sad day when you resort to a brothel or a bagel.

I read on their website that its sister café The Elephant House on George IV Bridge is frequented by Iain Rankin, Alexander McCall Smith and where J K Rowling wrote the first Harry Potter novel. But who needs to be flanked by hugely successful authors tapping away and sucking their pencils, when you can have bagels?

The bagels were great (although having written the joke in the first paragraph I couldn't face a

cream cheese and salmon one), but what I really liked was the art. When I first went there were loads of paintings of elephants by a musician and artist called John Hunt (online at johnhunt.org).

I loved them. They were colourful, cartoony and weird and they really appealed to the budding animator in me.

Quick Bites

FOOD

Every time I've won an award in Edinburgh I've used the prize money to buy one of John Hunt's paintings. I've got a red elephant (named Susan, by the artist—2001 New Comedy Award For Animation) and a Crocodile called Agatha—2003 Perrier Award Nomination).

When he was born I decorated my son's bedroom with them. Sadly when he reached four he confided in me that their googly eyes scared him, so now they're back under the bed (sorry, John).

RONNY CHIENG
// MINI FOOD GUIDE //

I visited Edinburgh for the first time in 2011 for the Edinburgh
Festival Fringe and was immediately enchanted by ancient city and the
cobblestone streets and the lack of dietary fibre. With this in mind, and in
no particular order, here is my top three list of favourite places to go to in
Edinburgh. Take note this list is based mainly on my lack of exploration
of the city any further than three blocks past where I was staying last year,
and so it is incredibly uninformed.

The Mosque Kitchen

THERE ARE DIETARY FIBRE AND VEGETABLES HERE, as
well as a Halal curry buffet at a reasonable price. The owner of the
establishment kindly gave me some unsolicited advice by telling me
to eat slower because the speed at which I eat is unhealthy. I do eat too
quickly BUT WHY DON'T YOU STICK TO COOKING THE FOOD
BUDDY? MAYBE I'M EATING QUICKLY BECAUSE YOUR SHIT IS
DELICIOUS?

Tupiniquim

Named some unpronounceable word, I just know it as the tiny little
street box store that somehow contains everything that is needed to cook
fresh crepes and is owned by native Brazilians. Brazilians! I asked why
they would trade Brazil for Edinburgh, because while Edinburgh is a
beautiful city in its own way, I think it is fair to say sunshine and beaches
is definitely not one of its strengths. They didn't have a good answer for
me, even after I pressed the issue and was asked to leave. The crepes and
smoothies were delicious and fresh. In a Festival that has no shortage of
crepe stalls, this permanent Edinburgh fixture is quite possible the best of
all of them.

The Elephant House

This is the cafe that JK Rowling supposedly sat in to write her first Harry
Potter book on napkins, which made her gazillions, AND BOY DO
THEY MILK THAT FOR ALL IT'S WORTH? They go on and on about
it. WE GET IT ELEPHANT HOUSE. She was broke when she started
writing her series here and now she's successful. Did you ever offer her any

coffee on the house back then? Or are you just riding her coattails right now? And why does your website end in .biz? I wonder if the cafe I'm writing this article in will put up a plaque about it one day.

JENNY BEDE
// CITY RESTAURANT //
City Restaurant, 35 Nicolson St, EH8 9BE. 0131 667 2819, thecityrestaurant.co.uk.
Daily 8am-1am.

When it comes to my favourite place to eat in Edinburgh, its a close toss up between the vegetarian restaurant David Bann and the City Restaurant. They are a bit different; David Bann enables me to follow my largely gluten- and sugar-free, technically vegan diet, whilst City Restaurant will deep fry your Nan if you ask nicely—and they can fit her in the fryer.

But it's also the place where dreams are made, if, like me, your dreams often consist of melted cheese on carbohydrates. If at any point during the festival the whole thing gets too tough, I will mostly likely be found at the back of the City Restaurant, mainlining a (large) cheesy chips and two battered sausages. Now, as I'm (technically) a gluten-free vegan, this kind of fare is usually disallowed, but as everyone knows, rules are different in Edinburgh. And vegan or no vegan, I bloody love me a battered sausage.

At the Adelaide Festival this year my boyfriend and I went to see Morgan & West's magic show. During it they ask the audience to think of an answer to the question: "What is your Achilles' heel... your one weakness?" They then picked someone from the audience and rather impressively guessed it.

Back at the apartment I asked my boyfriend what his answer had been, to which he incredibly sweetly replied: "You. Because I'd do anything for you. So that probably makes you my biggest weakness." Oh. "Why, what was yours?" he asked. Having been genuinely touched by his answer, I took his hand, looked deep into his expectant eyes, and said the three words that deep down he knew were coming: "a battered sausage."

BARBERSHOPERA

// GARIBALDI'S //

Garibaldi's, 97A Hanover St, EH2 1DJ. 0131 220 3007. Daily 6pm-3am.

The place I am going to talk about is a guilty pleasure, but it holds a dear place in my heart as we have ended up spending at least one crazy night there every year we have performed up at the Fringe!

From street level, Garibaldi's looks like your average Mexican restaurant... but by night, downstairs is an underground, sticky-walled club in New Town.

Complete with a light-up dance floor, pole and giant fan, Garibaldi's has all the ingredients for the best cheesy, trashy night of fun!

The music is pop and Latino mixed in with a few retro favourites—dare I say it, the Five Megamix medley is an embarrassing favourite!

> "...dare I say it, the Five Megamix medley is an embarrassing favourite!"

Throw in a few frozen margaritas and essential good company and you are in for a cracking night of silliness!

Not for those of you who fancy sipping martinis at a sleek bar (I am a fan of both) but for a fun, carefree night of dancing and laughter it is worth a visit! I heart Garibaldis!

WITTANK

// WANNABURGER //

Wannaburger, 7-8 Queensferry St, EH2 4PA. 0131 220 0036, wannaburger.com. Daily 11.30am-10pm.

One of our favourite places in Edinburgh is Wannaburger. It is more of a fully-franchised fast food outlet than a secret, but the WitTank-Wannaburger story is a tale of love.

When we first came to Edinburgh in 2006, we were instantly infatuated. Love at first bite, if that weren't such a hugely irritating cliché.

A regrettable hour of indigestion later, we knew we couldn't stay mad at those burgers for long, and so we kept going back.

Over the course of one particular meal, blood sugar levels through the roof, the joking suggestion emerged that were we ever to receive a 5-star review for our sketch show, we would return to Wannaburger and celebrate by each consuming one burger for every star awarded. Five burgers each.

The idea was brilliantly, thrillingly obscene in its conception, not least because in those days, the burgers in question were not far off the size of a human head.

Nowadays, the restaurant has relocated, forcing its patrons from the Old Town to at least earn their calorific goodness (not us—we get a cab). The burgers are also distinctly more manageable. So when our first 5-star review finally materialised in 2011, it satisfied more than one kind of hunger.

Quick Bites

FOOD

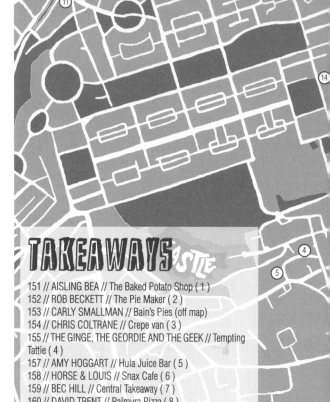

TAKEAWAYS

SWEET TOOTH

Foodies Festival

with top chefs

Edinburgh Inverleith Park

August 9, 10 & 11

MICHELIN STARRED CHEF **JEFF BLAND** COOKING LIVE

AISLING BEA
// THE BAKED POTATO SHOP //

The Baked Potato Shop, 56 Cockburn St, EH1 1PB. 0131 225 7572. Festival hours daily 11am-11pm.

There is nothing more humble than a potato. Even the working class parsnip seems arrogant in comparison to this starchy hero. It is quite literally down to earth and everyone can get along with it.

I come from a country that lost half of its population when we ran out of potatoes, leaving only a few hardy legends behind to sing about how difficult a spudless life was.

And so to The Baked Potato Shop. Inside this little Edinburgh gem are burly men, lancing giant baked potatoes from huge ovens and slapping them down in front of a deli counter full of toppings for you to choose with your piggy little fingers.

It's all veggie, but you would hardly notice. Their portions are f-off massive, so even a meat-eating 'I don't cry, I'm not a woman' beefcake will leave with his belly satisfied and balls intact. Their chilli will knock your orthopedic sandals off. I personally recommend going healthy and adding avocado, but you can also do an old school butter, beans and cheese.

Their prices are low, they stay open until 8pm and if you wrap up your leftover potato properly, it will still be hot when you come back from watching student theatre two hours later. The potato will not be the decision you regret from your day.

The drawback is that you often have to queue and that you can't sit down inside because they are small and popular like a Ford Ka. Be prepared to eat your steamy friend on the street or in your hotel. But there is something wonderful about sitting on a curb in Edinburgh, watching clowns wander by crying, while you horse a hot, filthy mess of mash into your face.

ROB BECKETT

// THE PIE MAKER //

38 South Bridge, EH1 1LL. 0131 558 1728, thepiemaker.co.uk.
Festival opening times Mon-Thu 9am-2am, Fri & Sat 9am-3am, Sun 10am-midnight.

It's not really that secret but it is still one of my favourite places to
visit when I need to cheer myself up when it is all cold and wet. So,
basically all the time in Edinburgh.

The Pie Maker on Nicholson Street is the Ronseal of the bakery
industry. Their branding is straight to the point with no messing
around; they make pies and they make them very well.

During my first Edinburgh I did a package show with a few other
comics, including Tom Rosenthal, to whom I am eternally grateful
for introducing me to The Pie Maker.

He would come in nearly every day with a pie for breakfast, which
I thought was just plain weird until one day I was so curious to
see what the big deal was that I had one too and became a pie-for-
breakfast man myself.

Along with pies, they also knock out a full range of other savoury
snacks which I enjoy at all times of the day: remember, The Pie
Maker is for life, not just for breakfast.

Just don't eat a sausage roll whilst walking in the rain, though; trying
to get soggy pastry out of clothing is an absolute nightmare.

CARLY SMALLMAN
// BAIN'S PIES //

John Bain & Son, 2 Stenhouse Cross, EH11 3JY. 0131 443 3177, johnbainedinburghltd.co.uk. Tue-Fri 8am-4.30pm, Sat 7am-1.30pm.

Do you like pies? Do you like delicious pies? Do you like places that are nowhere near the tourist trail, but feature the best pies you will ever encounter?

If the answer to these questions is 'yes' (or you are currently eating a sub-standard pie) then I simply have to recommend to you one of the greatest hidden gems in the whole of Edinburgh.

If you take the number 22 bus out of town you will end up at my Granny's flat in Stenhouse Cross. My granny is awesome—but not as awesome as the pies that can be found in Bain's the Butchers, the shop underneath her house. It's a bit of a journey from the city centre, but well worth it.

People queue round the block when the butchers opens because the pies are that good. Did I mention that I love pies?? Forget the castle. Forget Holyrood Palace. Forget Arthur's Seat. It's all about Bain's pies.

CHRIS COLTRANE
// CREPE VANS & GRAVEYARDS //

The Cafe Crepe van will move around the C venues during the Fringe in 2013. Contact them via facebook.com/cafecrepesltd

If I'm being truthful, my favourite place in Edinburgh is the crepe van by the Gilded Balloon, because ON THREE OCCASIONS I've convinced the staff there to put an entire, industrial-sized, 750g tub of Nutella on my pancake.

Have you ever heard of such beauty? It wobbles like an unstable jelly that has evolved sentience, and wants to start putting the world to rights. I could have teamed up with it to fight crime, but sadly for you I ate it. Good luck trying to fix this mess of a country on your own, losers.

But, as I'm doing a political comedy show, I should try to cultivate an air of intellectualism, so let's go just down the road from Bistro Square, to Greyfriars Kirk graveyard.

Not only is it a very calming place for ex-goths like me to get away from the frantic festival and to write while surrounded by some impressive funerary art, but it also has significant history: the National Covenant was signed there in 1638, an important moment in Scottish independence from England in which they demanded free Scottish parliament and a free General Assembly, without interference from the King.

It is also the home to the statue of Greyfriars Bobby, the dog who was said to have guarded his owner's grave for 14 years, until he died. Plus you will sometimes see me there, which is probably the most culturally significant thing about it.

Luckily you are allowed in even if, like me, you're a filthy god-loathing atheist. Make an effort to pop in when you need some thinking time, or if you want to impress hot dudes and chicks by reading poetry under a tree.

THE GINGE, THE GEORDIE AND THE GEEK

// TEMPTING TATTIE //

Tempting Tattie, 18 Jeffrey St, EH1 1DT. 0131 556 7960.
Mon-Sat noon-5.30pm.

The one place you are guaranteed to find the Ginge, the Geordie, the Geek, or even all three at the same time throughout Edinburgh, is the Tempting Tattie.

With haggis and coleslaw on the Ginge's tattie, a blend of coronation and sweet chilli chicken on the Geordie's and a spade load of tuna on a wee tattie for the 'Atkins' enthusiast Geek, they cater for all.

The only downside to this magnificent establishment is that the boys' pants get tighter throughout the month, creating the rather distinct muffin tops come the end of August.

Rose Street in the New Town is home to a plethora of places to catch a quick bite to eat.

AMY HOGGART

// HULA JUICE BAR //

Hula, 103-105 West Bow, EH1 2JP. 0131 220 1121, hulajuicebar.co.uk. Daily 8am-late.

My favourite place in Edinburgh is Hula Juice Bar, just off Grassmarket. Mae Martin recommended it to me as she said the staff were great: she fancied one of the waitresses and said another looked like a white Rihanna. As a result, she spent thousands there over the course of the month.

She also got me hooked, and I probably spent the same amount on pretentious juices with fruit and vegetables in them. Even if you hate your show, you're doing it on the Free Fringe to an average of no audience, you're not sleeping, you're drinking far too much and eating crap, I guarantee you can feel good about yourself every day if you buy a Ginger Jack juice from Hula.

Make sure you ask for extra carrot and spinach if they have it, one of those organic immune booster shots, extra multi-vitamins (what does that even mean?), antioxidants and anything else they have that doesn't taste very nice.

My rule is: if the drink turns green or better yet brown, you know you are getting something right this August. And they also do genuinely yummy food. Plus you can hang out with me and Mae.

157

HORSE & LOUIS

// SNAX CAFE //

Snax Cafe, West Register St. 0131 557 8688, snaxcafe.com. Mon-Fri 6.30am-5pm, Sat 7am-5pm, Sun 7.30am-5pm. Also on Buccleuch St. 0131 662 9009. Mon-Fri 7am-5pm, Sat 7am-6pm, Sun 8am-6pm.

Like many comedians who have experienced a fair few Fringes, our time in Edinburgh is dominated by a very basic set of emotions: total physical exhaustion, hangover-induced bodily anguish and constant, gnawing hunger.

All of these problems can be solved by a brief visit to Snax Cafe on West Register Street. Here you will find that elusive 'real Edinburgh', ie people who don't give a shit about the Fringe and definitely don't want one of your effing flyers.

The clientele are real people, working people, people who are genuinely looking for chicken curry with a side of haggis at 6.30am and who expect, nay demand, that every meal comes with chips (non-negotiable). These are people who have heard of salad but wouldn't recognise it if it was tossed all over their faces.

For us, nothing beats a hangover into submission better than a bacon and egg roll and a cappuccino. Except, that is, a bacon and egg roll that costs just £1.80 and a cappuccino for a mere £1.50. And don't be thinking this is some sort of limp-wristed, mini-roll breakfast snack. This is bacon so thick you could use it as a door stop, and an egg that, if hard boiled, would do some damage down a ten-pin lane.

A brief word of warning, though: if you, like us, leave the house in the morning and don't go home again until you can't stand for exhaustion, or can't find anyone to carry on drinking with you (when does that ever happen?), then that first bite is all-important.

Get it wrong and for the rest of the day no-one will be listening to your flyering spiel or talking to you as a human being; they will be pointing out the egg yolk all over your t-shirt/jumper/kagool and saying how delicious it looks. That's ingrained advertising for the glory of Snax Cafe.

FOOD

Takeaways

BEC HILL

// CENTRAL TAKEAWAY //

Central Takeaway, 15-16 Teviot Place, EH1 2QZ. 0131 226 6898. Daily 11.30am-1.45am, Sun-Thu 4.30pm-1.30am, Fri & Sat 4.30pm-3am.

BATTERED CHEESEBURGER

(WRONG, BUT SO RIGHT)

by Bec Hill

If I ever sell out, I treat myself to a battered cheeseburger from the chippy on Teviot Place. I like how the walls are completely covered in show posters. I feel surrounded by photos of famous comedians, my friends and the occasional act who thinks Comic Sans is a perfectly reasonable font choice.

I like to sit on one of the high stools at the front window and watch the families and eager punters head towards the venues. Or the performers and staff trudging home with a plastic Tesco bag and a pocketful of dreams.

It is the one moment I allow myself to feel completely content. At that moment, I feel successful. I feel satisfied. I feel happy and full of greasy, meaty, cheesy deliciousness. Usually, it is raining and I'm thankful to be sitting in the warm glow of the neon light in the window. Dry. Safe. Smug.

But, as soon as the last bite of that deep-fried delicacy is gone, it all vanishes. Suddenly, I realise: I'm in a dingy chip shop, with questionable customers, and I will never be as good as I want to be. I look up at the faces on the posters around me. They stare at the empty polystyrene box and judge me. I feel sick. With a heavy heart, I step out into the rain and head to the overpriced student flat I call 'home' for August. (But not before leaving a pile of flyers for my show on the counter.) Maybe there is a plus side to not selling out, after all.

Takeaways

FOOD

159

DAVID TRENT

MY SHOW IS ALWAYS A LATE NIGHTER SO I DON'T EVEN START THINKING ABOUT FOOD UNTIL AFTER MIDNIGHT. AS A RESULT OF THIS I ENDED UP SHOVING KEBABS FROM PALMYRA INTO MY FACE FOR 21 NIGHTS STRAIGHT LAST YEAR. EVERY NIGHT-TASTY AS FUCK. I CAN'T BELIEVE THAT THIS PLACE CAN REALLY QUALIFY AS SECRET AS IT HAS QUEUES EVERY NIGHT BUT IF YOU HAVEN'T BEEN, YOU HAVEN'T BEEN... WHEN I GOT BACK FROM EDINBURGH I WAS DIAGNOSED WITH NON ALCOHOLIC FATTY LIVER DISEASE AND ENDED UP IN HOSPITAL. SO. PALMYRA PIZZA KEBAB.

RICHARD VRANCH

// CAFE PICCANTE //

Cafe Piccante, 19 Broughton St, 0131 478 7884, cafepiccante.com. Sun-Thu 4pm-3am, Fri & Sat 4pm-4am.

Broughton Street seemed pleasant enough when I first performed at the Edinburgh Fringe in 1979.

Since then it has blossomed. There are trendy cafes, a great wine shop and the wet fish shop survives. There's been a health food shop since vegetables were legalised in Scotland in 1997.

Cafe Piccante sits right at the top of Broughton Street. It sells gorgeous fast food and it is open very late, just when you're staggering home from that Fringe venue club bar. Edinburgh nights are unmistakable. The smell of the brewery, the scream of bagpipes, the feel of the flyers. You notice a neon sign advertising deep fried Mars bars and soon you're inside. It's not just Edinburgh any more, it's Edinburgh Piccante. It's bright, it's busy. Sometimes there's a live DJ on the decks in the corner. A lot of Fringe venues aren't as much fun as this.

I probably eat more fast food during August than I do the rest of the year. Most of it is from Cafe Piccante; it's irresistible. The range is bewildering so normally I stick to old favourites:

Fish, chips and beer. Better than fish and chips, to the tune of beer. That's a balanced lunch, let alone a snack. Chips with cheese and gravy. Sounds simple. Could anybody make it? I'm not sure. The simplest ingredients transcend to a higher level when nuanced by experts in their field.

The following day you might find yourself unable to get up before Pointless. No problem. Cafe Piccante not only has a website, but also an iPhone app you can download to upload food direct to your door. And the portions are not small. Arriba!

Palmyra Pizza, 22 Nicolson St, EH8 9DH. 0131 667 6655. Festival hours midday-5am.

Takeaways

FOOD

ERIC LAMPEART

// CHEESEE PEASEE //

Cheesee Peasee. 01875 340912, cheesee-peasee.com. Check website for details and latest timetable.

There is a stench that can make your stomach twitch, and your skin itch, if you're allergic to dairy. But the same can be an aroma that can quench and whet your appetite for something not battered and Scottish. 'Twixt Meadow Place and Leamington Walk, every Saturday, there stands the culprit for your dancing nostrils: a truck is parked and full of cheese.

Inside the white vessel—named the Cheesy Peasee—this rosy-cheeked Cousteau named Cedric will greet you. A French-born (Lyon, to be specific) Edinburgh resident will trade you slabs of fromage for British money.

He doesn't take euros; I tried. And if you impress him with his native tongue, he'll (probably) slice you an extra 50 grams of Camembert. Merci beaucoup: thanks a lot.

Merci beau cul: thanks, nice arse. He'll love that! "75 grams of Roule coming right up!"

Everyone from miles around comes to seek cheese guidance from this Gouda guru. And not just humans—I once took a knee by his Wensleydale wagon, while munching on a chunk of Stilton, to watch two Scottish seagulls (their squawks had a hint of Glaswegian) fight over a slice of edam, as if it were bird heroin.

I watched them for a good hour; possibly the funniest thing I saw at the Fringe that year. Five stars.

Either treat your inner French and head to the cheese wizard of the Meadow and trade him silver for tastebud gold.

Then pop to the off-licence, grab a bottle of vino and picnic yourself silly in the park. Or play hide and seek with him around the city. Here's a clue: follow your nose.

FELICITY WARD
// CHEESEE PEASEE //

If there's one thing that reminds me of the Edinburgh Fringe, it's comfort eating. Those feelings are going to eat themselves, are they? And a great way to seem sophisticated while you're chowing down on some self-loathing is doing it with a wheel of cheese.

Down the bottom of Marchmont Road, on the other side of The Meadows, is a van. And in the van is a French man. And in the man… well, he sells cheese.

Cheese that I can't pronounce. Cheese that stinks but tastes amazing. Cheese that I eat like I'm in a competition.

He's there every Saturday between 10am and 6pm. He lets you try different ones too, with the smug confidence of knowing you're about to buy your bodyweight in whatever you put into your gob.

And if all that isn't enough, the name of the van is: Cheesee Peasee. IT'S CHEESE, GUYS! PUNNY CHEESE!

If you still don't want to go there, then we have nothing in common and I'm sorry for your loss.

FRI	**North Berwick in front of Locketts Bros wine shop from 5pm to 7.30pm**
SAT	**Meadow place, Edinburgh 10am to 6pm**
SUN	**Stockbridge Market (corner of Saunders Street and Kerr Street)**

JAMES ACASTER
// FUDGE KITCHEN //

Fudge Kitchen, 30 High St, Royal Mile, EH1 1TB. 0131 558 1517, fudgekitchen.co.uk.
Daily 10am-6pm.

My favourite place to pop into in Edinburgh is the Fudge Kitchen on the Royal Mile. They have free samples on the counter. I am a big fan of free samples as I expect anyone else is. If you are not then I can't imagine why.

They make the fudge in the shop and you can watch them do it. This is fascinating and makes you want to eat the fudge, and thanks to the free samples you can—straight away.

The staff are very friendly and will not only tell you about fudge but also display a genuine interest in how you are emotionally, which you don't get just anywhere.

They wear green aprons and green is and always has been my favourite colour—hands down.

For the past couple of years the kitchen has also doubled up as a venue and they have had comedy shows on later in the day. I don't know if they are doing it this year but if they are then performances are always a joy and have a different feel to anything else due to being in a fudge shop.

Did I already mention the free samples?

Sweet Tooth

FOOD

DOC BROWN

// CHOCO-LATTE //

Choco-Latte, 39 South Clerk St, EH8 9NZ. 0131 667 0091, choco-latte.co.uk. Mon-Fri 10am-6pm, Sat & Sun 10am-6.30pm.

When I was about six years old my dad slipped me a chunk of what I initially assumed was crumbly fudge. It was buttery, almost sickeningly sweet, but with a melt in the mouth texture that I found completely irresistible. I had no idea then, but it was actually a piece of proper Scotch tablet, and it would be another 20 barren years before I tasted this manna again.

Fast forward to summer 2008 and I had been doing stand up for six months. I had been given the opportunity to perform as part of the Pleasance's Comedy Reserve for new comics and was being put up in some student-like digs behind South Clerk Street.

Having had a long affiliation with fudge, particularly Cornish, I'd heard there was a place on the Royal Mile that did good stuff. It was amazing in there, but… no tablet. Possibly reacting to the abject disgust on my face, the staff told me if I wanted real proper, genuine melt-in-ya-mouth-give-you-a-sugar-related-coronary tablet, I had to venture to a little known spot way down South Clerk Street. From whence I'd come!

I was off like a shot and walked so far I almost gave up, thinking the place must have closed down or something, but then I saw it. Now let me tell you this, unequivocally: there are some great 'ye olde' sweet shops in Edinburgh—Mr Simms et al—but Choco-Latte is no sweet shop. It's a flipping grotto.

It's the mecca of sugary goods. It's a pilgrimage for those with syrupy veins who worship the Candy Gods at the Choco Church. You can barely walk in there—there are bags of sweets hanging from the ceiling, goods bursting off the shelves—it's mental.

And just when you think you have got the place sussed, you realize that they also serve amazing coffee and unique homemade cakes—I mean proper bespoke cake making—crazy combos of sweets and chocolates mixed into pastries and sponges… and of course, crumbly, mouth watering, orgasmic Scotch Tablet.

Mass hysteria! I was high for a week. I nearly died of self abuse. And five years on, I'm coming back to finish the job. May I rest in sweet, buttery peace.

FLISS RUSSELL
// CHOCOLATE LOUNGE //

Chocolate Lounge, Harvey Nichols, 34 St Andrews Square, EH2 2AD. 0131 524 8300, chocolate-lounge.co.uk. Mon-Wed 10am-6pm, Thu-Sat 10am-9pm, Sun 11am-6pm.

My top tip for Secret Edinburgh is something I discovered last year and I will definitely be doing again this year. It is perfect for a girly getaway from all the festivities.

On the fourth floor of Harvey Nichols there is a little bar with a sushi-style conveyor belt. But instead of raw fish moving slowly past, there are mini-champagne bottles and cakes!

You sit around the bar and choose what you like from the belt. It is not especially expensive and you can sit there as long as you like, sipping your champagne and enjoying a delicious pudding.

Chocolate Lounge is perfect if you have something to celebrate or someone you really want to treat. I will be heading up there at least once this August and I can't wait.

FOOD

© Simone Eisath

OUT OF TOWN

168

// MARK THOMAS // Cycling to North Berwick
// ANDREW MAXWELL // Duddingston Village
// STEVE SHANYASKI // Musselburgh Beach
// PAT BURTSCHER // The Highlands
// JESSICA FOSTEKEW // Portobello Beach
// PHIL NICHOL // Lobster Shack
// DAVID WHITNEY // Cramond

ROB ROUSE
// GULLANE BAY //

During a hectic and heady month up in Edinburgh, you could do a lot worse than to get on a bus or a train and take a trip up the coast to Gullane Bay.

I'm not sure where they go from or at what times, but I'm banking on the fact you can work it out for yourself. We're comedians, not travel agents. You've probably got a smartphone anyway, or if you haven't, just ask people—they'll know.

Jesus, it's how we survived when I started gigging, fifteen years ago, driving sat-nav-less to the edge of some town in the arse end of nowhere and just asking. That way you meet people, you get to know where you are.

"I highly recommend it. I did it. I nearly died from the cold..."

Sometimes those people will get in your car and direct you straight to the gig because they're going there too. Other times they won't have a fucking clue where they're going and one awful occasion they might even wet themselves in your car.

Anyway, when you get to Gullane Bay you can fart around in the rock pools, have fish and chips on the sand, or if you really want to grow a pair, you can go for a swim in the North Sea. I highly recommend it. I did it. I nearly died from the cold. So I don't recommend it, but at the same time I do, it was kind of lovely and kind of awful all at the same time.

If you don't fancy that, then what better way to see Edinburgh, than on a bike?! In August, there's barely any traffic and very few pedestrians—so you can enjoy her completely flat and not at all hilly, un-cobbled streets on your two-wheeled steed.

DANA ALEXANDER
// ARTHUR'S SEAT //

© Orange Aurouchs

Arthur's Seat. It's not really a secret as it is a giant mountain. But with all the shows, parties (booze) and elderly people down below you would be surprised how many people actually can't physically make it up there. That's not to say that it's a strenuous hike, but you have to have the beer at the top.

The secret is to go up there before sunrise, which is early, but you are more than likely to be up there alone. When the sun finally rises you will have a great view of the city and the lake (or loch!)

It can be quite cold up there at that time so bring a jacket. If you choose to go up there in afternoon you will see other tourists, but it's relatively spacious and it is easy enough to get a bit of grass to sit on. I'd bring a tarp as the grass is likely to be wet.

The good thing about a bird's-eye view of the city is that it's a great way to see what's going on in Edinburgh. I saw a great food fest which I would never have known about if I hadn't gone up there. And then I ate half a pig.

I have been doing the Fringe for
years but 2011 was the first time
that I went up Arthur's Seat. It
annoyed me muchly that I had
wasted five years without walking
up its steep back.

I actually went up there to do a
stand-up gig. It is held on one day
of the festival every year and I
cannot wait to do it again this
year.

I remember it rained so much on
the week leading up to it I thought
it must be cancelled, but on the
day the sun shone relentlessly and
everyone just enjoyed a picnic and
watched me and Josie Long tell
stories on

p of a mountain.

felt like Frodo in Lord of the
ings, but instead of Mount Doom,
rthur's Seat; and instead of a
ng, a microphone; and instead
Samwise Gamgee, a compere...
kay, it was nothing like Lord of
e Rings. JOEL DOMMETT

The best place to clear my head is at the top of Arthur's Seat. It has the best view of the city, whilst reminding me that there is something else apart from comedy, for that one month. I head up there with Celia Pacquola every year; it has become a tradition, especially writing stupid words with the stones and then photographing ourselves laying next to the words. This is possibly the reason that I don't have a lot of friends. FELICITY WARD

THE HIGHEST COMED

IN AID OF
Save the Children

STEWART FRANCIS

TERRY ALDERTON

CRAIG CAMPBE

GLENN WOOL

SIMON EVANS

www.theaidfundraiser.c
 @aidfundraiser

DAN NIGHTINGALE

// THE HILL WITH NO NAME //

Behind Marchmont Road, out past the Meadows at the south side of Edinburgh, where I stay when I am at the festival, there's a hill with the Royal Observatory at the top. It's less well known than Arthur's Seat, but it is always quieter.

Sometimes I try to run up it; most times I just walk to the top. It is where I head of an afternoon to clear my head and detach myself from the festival.

"...I watched a rain storm sweep over the city from the coast and quietly chuckled to myself..."

I have a sit and watch the city, knowing all the madness of the Fringe is going on below—but not being able to hear anything but the wind rushing in from the Firth is a hugely relaxing feeling.

The last time I was there, I watched a rain storm sweep over the city from the coast and quietly chuckled to myself, thinking of all the flyer teams getting drenched, the tourists ducking into Free Fringe shows for cover rather than culture, and the comedians heading to their venues cursing the Edinburgh weather.

Then it started raining and I got wet, which I supposed I deserved, though really I didn't mind.

I don't actually know the name of the hill but I suppose I don't need to. I know where it is.

JOHN FLEMING

// BLACKFORD HILL //

I can tell Dan Nightingale that his hill is Blackford Hill, just south of Morningside. When I was newly 18, I tried to commit suicide with pills. This was a bad idea because I had always been shit at Chemistry in school.

I was persuaded to go into a mental home in Essex, because I had tried to kill myself. I did. But I only stayed two days and one night because they kept asking me questions when I just wanted to be alone.

I went back to my distraught parents' home, but it was no better there. Not their fault. So I ran away from home.

I hitched to Edinburgh which was and is my favourite British city. Ever since I was an embryo, I had gone there once a year with my parents to spend a few days with my father's aunt, who lived in Morningside.

When I ran away to Edinburgh, I slept one night in a multi-storey car park at the foot of the castle rock. I spent another sleeping in the stairwell of a block of flats. It was very cold.

In Morningside, I saw my great aunt shopping on the other side of the street. I did not talk to her.

Later, I walked up Blackford Hill at twilight. The city was spread out before me, the castle rising up in the distance on the left; Arthur's Seat rising up in the distance on the right. The waters of the Forth were twinkling in the background with Fife beyond them; the lights of the twilight city were starting to twinkle in the foreground.

It was totally peaceful and now, every time I go to Edinburgh for the Fringe, at least once I walk up Blackford Hill to feel that tranquility amidst the anarchy.

JOE LYCETT

// BRAID BURN //

My favourite place in Edinburgh is the route along the Braid Burn stream, to the south of the city. In recent years I have taken, quite fervently, to recreational running, and the path down the Braid Burn is one of the most tranquil and beautiful places I have ever had the fortune to run through.

The Fringe is a terribly long month and yet also a fleeting affair. On the one hand the expectation to be entertaining relentlessly every evening seems at first like it will never end, but such sensational things happen and you meet so many remarkable people that by the end you wonder how you squeezed so much in.

Running for me is a form of meditation; an opportunity to recall and process the things that have happened. When I am short for time I do a couple of laps of the Meadows, a perfectly agreeable place to run. But when I really want to escape, just running a little further south brings you into a hidden oasis of natural beauty. A gentle stream of water dances between the trees that tower over you from both sides. In August the wood is full of summer bloom, green and lush and full of life; expect the occasional fallen oak. At one point you pass a small cottage hidden away amongst some bushes, before finally emerging to the west and reconnecting with the Meadows for the last stretch. Then I shower, dress and begin another day of bonkers fun at the Edinburgh Fringe festival.

I was introduced to the Braid Burn by fellow comedian Rob Deering. He is a fantastic runner and much quicker than I. If you are a thief I would recommend choosing to mug someone other than Rob, as he would definitely give you a run for his money.

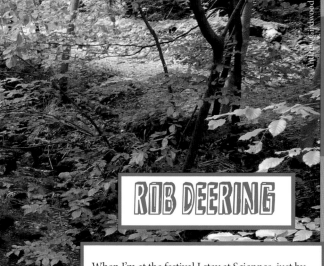

© Andrew Charlwood

ROB DEERING

When I'm at the festival I stay at Sciennes, just by the end of the Meadows—it is super-handy for all the big venues, but every couple of days I run off in the opposite direction, south away from town and then west along a gorgeous little valley towards Morningside—Blackford Glen and the Hermitage of Braid, past the Braid Burn.

Braid Burn bubbles and tumbles its way down through the woods like something out of an old novel—actually, it is mentioned in the Prime of Miss Jean Brodie, although I was thinking longer ago than that—and the whole scene is so pretty and pastoral it puts every last poster, flyer and little-black-box-studio-space out of your mind for a minute.

Pretty wet down there though. They've spent millions on flood defences the last few years, but they wouldn't have had to if it wasn't, y'know, like, really wet, eh.

181

JAY FOREMAN
// CALTON HILL //

Arthur's Seat towers smugly over Edinburgh, thinking to itself how popular and brilliant it is. But just because it is the highest point in the city, doesn't necessarily make it the best view. For my money, Calton Hill, its little brother about a mile to the north is a much worthier trip than Arthur's Seat, and here's why:

1. Calton Hill is only a four-minute walk away from the corner of Princes Street, and only about fifty steps to reach the top. So unlike Arthur's Seat, you can pop up there for a quickie at a moment's notice. This makes it a perfect escape from the festival for the elderly, the tired, or the fat.

2. Calton Hill is littered with bizarre 18th-century monuments to sit on, including a cannon, an observatory that looks like a telescope and three enormous, useless walls with pillars that were supposed to become a temple before they ran out of money. It gives the place a wonderful air of pointlessness.

3. You are in the centre of the city and much closer to the sea than Arthur's Seat, which means you get a completely different view from every angle. To the west you can see straight down the middle of Princes Street and race buses from one end to the other; to the north all of New Town and the Firth of Forth; and to the south, something you certainly don't get from Arthur's Seat: Arthur's Seat itself! You can even clearly make out silhouettes marching like lemmings to the top of Arthur's Seat. Fools.

I go up Calton Hill as often as I can to escape from the festival, and for the awesome unrivalled sense of scale you get up there. People mill around in the streets below, and without even turning your head, you can also see the coastline you'll recognise from the map. Pop up there if you ever need reminding how small we all are. And to make the experience all the more complete, reward yourselves when you get to the top with a cheeky doobie!

ROBIN AND PARTRIDGE

// CALTON HILL //

Secrets don't always mean going to the back of beyond. I've heard a few stories from friends who've travelled about, escaping to the slopes of Machu Picchu, or hiking through Bhutan, or smoking peace-pipes with the tree-dwelling wicker folk of New Guinea, only for them suddenly to spot someone they were at uni with. Voyaging halfway round the work and failing to escape your demographic is one of travel's crueler punchlines. I guess that's the point of 'secrets'.

In Edinburgh one year, when a friend's (brilliant!) show was being seen by an average of two people a day (including his techie), he was haemorrhaging cash. On top of this metaphorical mugging by the festival, he had also literally been mugged, so we decided to take a perspective-shifting walk up Arthur's Seat. At the summit, amid the wind and bluster, we ran into not one, but two comedians who had just been nominated for awards. Of course, hearty congratulations were exchanged and we ended up walking back with one of them, but it wasn't quite the distance we were hoping for. It would seem Arthur's Seat is no secret either—city centre national parks rarely are.

The path less well trodden is Calton Hill. It's a world heritage site like Machu Picchu, but there isn't a leavers' hoodie in sight. My favourite time to come here is 5am to watch the sunrise over Leith from the forgotten National Monument: the Acropolis. This Victorian neo-classical façade is part of a building that was never finished and sits fenced off amidst a tangle of nettles and buddleias. It doesn't match the rugged beauty of Arthur's Seat, but there's a dynamic feel to the nature here. It's fighting back!

Also near the Acropolis is a not-so-ancient standing stone from the noughties, celebrating the founding of the Scottish Parliament. It is called something like 'The Rock of Scotland'. If this all seems vague and poorly researched, it's because I cannot seem to find this stone on maps or any mention of it online, but it IS there. So how secret is that?

KIERAN HODGSON

NEWHAVEN // LOCH FYNE // HARBOUR INN

Every year during the Fringe a glorious day comes. Mum and Dad, who visit the Fringe mainly for jazz concerts, will take me to dinner, often as a way of cheering me up after another of my underwhelming and mediocre performances.

For years we experimented: Italian, curry, pub food, but nothing quite hit the spot. Then one day it clicked – Tesco vouchers. With the finest chain restaurants in the land opening up to us as never before, the search for the best brought us to one of the city's most charming, tranquil and just bloody pleasant places – Newhaven, in Leith.

Loch Fyne Seafood Restaurant occupies one half of the colossal old fish market hall, and overlooks a small, sheltered harbour still full of gently bobbing vessels. Of a quiet Tuesday evening you watch the sun set behind the Forth Bridge and that whole Fringe scene (crying into your flyers on the Mile by day, crying into your cider in Pleasance Dome by night) drifts away as you tuck into pan-fried sea bream and steal a forkful of Mum's shellfish risotto. It makes you glad to be alive and nauseatingly middle class.

And the fun doesn't stop there. There's the bus ride down along Leith Walk, of course, and Lothian Buses' aggressive Exact Change Only policy means you just have to break a tenner in the Harbour Inn before making the journey home.

The walls are covered with sea charts and fishing paraphernalia, the Deuchars isn't £4.50 a pint, and if it's a warm evening you can stand outside and gaze across the Firth of Forth to the ports and hills of Fife, far in the distance. You couldn't come here every day during the Fringe, but for that one precious evening it's the most magical place –

MAX DICKINS

// NEWHAVEN //

The trawler men who dock at Newhaven are among the funniest people in the world. I remember when I first came across them. It was midway through the festival last year.

I accidentally wandered into a mackerel-eating competition at 2am, blind drunk. I'd just been to see a Plymouth University production of Zumba the Musical, and had been so bored that I drank eight bottles of gin to numb the pain.

Desperately trying to find a kebab shop, I got awfully lost and ended up at the harbour. I'm so glad I did. The fishermen regaled me with an astonishing array of fishy gags, amusing crustacean anecdotes, and surreal non-sequiturs. "Why did the clam cross the road? Who cares? The English are stealing our North Sea oil revenues."

I was impressed. At the time my show was struggling. A child from Three Weeks had reviewed it as 'a complete pile of wank', three stars. So I desperately asked the trawlermen for help. We worked through the night on my script, staying awake on a cocktail of adrenaline and whelks. But it was worth it. After the fishermen's help, audience numbers went through the roof, and the reviews were amazing.

Chortle described it as 'the best hour of lobster related story-telling I've ever heard'. Bruce Dessau at the Evening Standard said that I had 'scaled the heights', stealing one of the best puns from the show. The fish chef Rick Stein came eight nights in a row, I'd never been so arousing.

That Edinburgh opened a lot of doors for me. I have since recorded the pilot of my new deep-sea chat show Fish and Quips, and I've even managed to go part time at the brothel. And it's all down to my fishermen friends: thank you, Newhaven Harbour.

MARK THOMAS
// CYCLING TO NORTH BERWICK //

My secret Edinburgh is not in Edinburgh so this article is either mis-titled (making it the publisher's fault) or inappropriate (making it mine).

My secret Edinburgh is North Berwick, a place best visited by cycle. It is easily found; head to Leith, turn right at the water for some 20 to 25 miles, and you can't miss it.

The downhill journey from the Playhouse towards the docks passes over some of the worst-kept road in Europe; the surface is scarred with cobbles, ruts, pothole and debris most commonly seen after small-scale civil war. So gird your loins and arse for this part as it can be a haemorrhoid-inducing jaunt.

Turn right at the docks, go through Portobello (a great seaside town with a brilliant swimming pool), past Musselburgh, follow the

shoreline, up an inhaler-inducing hill by the golf course and some two to three hours after setting out, you will be in North Berwick.

If you want a temporary escape from the sometimes insular world of the Edinburgh festival, nothing quite does the job like fish and chips by the seaside after a cycle. In fact, get yourself an ice cream—you deserve it.

One of my favourite days during any festival was visiting the Highland Games in North Berwick. What is not to like? Fairground rides, pipe bands, big things being thrown, the sun out, fish and chips, all good in their own right but together...

And as for the pipe bands, forget the annoying piper down at Waverley station; I would put money that even the hardest cynic could not witness the pipe bands and feel the hairs on the back of their neck twitch a little.

© Mike Quinn

ANDREW MAXWELL
// DUDDINGSTON VILLAGE //

At least once a week during the festival I climb Arthur's Seat either alone or I take people up there too. But climb up to the top and then down the south side, away from the city and you come down into Duddingston Village, which is nestled in the valley and completely hidden from the city.

It's a cobbled street village and in the heart of the village is one of the oldest pubs in Scotland, called The Sheep Heid Inn.

Once you've climbed over the hill and got there you can sit in leather armchairs and simply get away from the world.

It's beautiful, it has a beer garden, it serves food and it has a skittle alley. And the pub has taken part in many of the biggest and most dramatic events in Scottish history.

A lot of the plots against Scottish kings, the overthrows and regal intrigue, took place within that building.

© Lamda

STEVE SHANYASKI

// MUSSELBURGH BEACH //

There's a beach up past Musselburgh which I always drive to during the Festival. It's the absolute opposite to the Fringe—solitary, silent, and visually expansive.

I go running up there usually, or just walk about picking up shells for the house back in England. It's always quite windy, but just a great place to go and get away from the chaos of the Fringe.

Being able to walk two miles without a single flyer for an improvised comedy troupe being thrust towards you is as close to heaven as possible in August.

PAT BURTSCHER
// THE HIGHLANDS //

I really don't want to because then it might turn into something that I don't like. But on the other hand, that vegetarian restaurant that I loved is now a noodle bar that I hate. So I hope that this creates enough buzz to keep the place in business, and not have it overrun with yahoos and/or noodles!

So that special place that I love and cherish and look forward to going to every time I'm in and around Edinburgh, but am a bit anxious about sharing with you (reader), because it might fill up with noodles, is the Highlands. There are funny cows there.

One in particular, named

Shamus, is ultra famous! You can also walk around in nature and enjoy it for the beautiful thing it is, and remember that that is where we are supposed to be!

Not trapped at work, but sleeping in fields and chasing butterflies for breakfast! So if

you go there, enjoy it and don't be a douchebag (someone who messes it up for other people).

Oh, and tell Shamus I said hello!

Snapdragon Productions
with Damian Arnold
presents

Thark

by **Ben Travers**

Adapted by
Clive Francis
Directed by
Eleanor Rhode

A rip-roaring
revival of the clas
Aldwych Farce

21 August–
22 September 2013

PARK

Tickets: **parktheatre.co.**
Phone: 020-7870 6876
⊖ Finsbury Park

SNAPDRAGON
PRODUCTIONS

JERWOOD **SPACE**

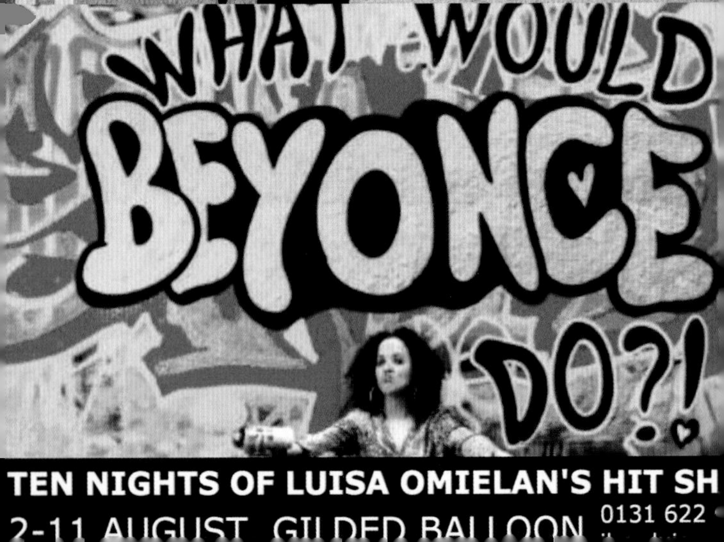

WHAT WOULD BEYONCE DO?!

TEN NIGHTS OF LUISA OMIELAN'S HIT SH
2-11 AUGUST GILDED BALLOON
0131 622

JESSICA FOSTEKEW
// PORTOBELLO BEACH //

I grew up in Swanage, a grey, dated and desolate seaside town in Dorset. The sort where the sulky beach was usually quiet but for a few ancient souls, lounging their way ever closer to death in their deckchairs, with hankies on their heads.

The sort of place where tourists get frowned at and whispered about, a permanent source of twitching, fear and suspicion, despite providing the town's only real income.

The sort of place that you wouldn't call 'pretty' but it stank of nostalgia. The penny arcades, the tacky tat and the simplicity of it; bleak, almost sinister, yet somehow charming.

The sort of place you can bound in and sea-swim all year round, the colder the better, to really, truly remind yourself you're alive… then shudder back out, frozen, happy and deserving the incredible freshly-caught fish with freshly-caught chips you get with a mug of tea and bread and butter in a shorefront gingham-coated café.

So Portobello, just outside Edinburgh city centre, is my favourite place to escape from the festival.

It is identical to my first home. It won't be to everyone's liking—it's basically a freaky wee beach. But for me it's like crawling back into the womb.

PHIL NICHOL

// LOBSTER SHACK - NORTH BERWICK //

North Berwick Harbour. 07910 620 480, lobstershack.co.uk. Summer hours noon-8pm.

Go to Edinburgh Waverley and get on a two-carriage train to North Berwick, running once an hour. Go to the end of the line, just past Musselburgh. Walk down to the beautiful big beach, and walk all around the marina, past the bird and seal sanctuary, past a children's lido and a walled-off portion of the sea where you can swim and see a view over the Grampians. Walk along the beach from where the bird tours leave, around the sea wall, and you come to the Lobster Shack.

It's a tiny little caravan doing lobsters, half-lobsters and mussels and chips. You can sit on their chairs or along the sea wall to see the sea. They have got a wine list and do catch-of-the-days, all from this tiny caravan. The guys also run a hotel in town so there's a good hotel chef doing the cooking.

I can't remember who gave us the hint. One year, my girlfriend

Christy and I met in London just before Edinburgh and I invited her up. She came up and we went down to Fishers Bistro in Leith for the oysters at the end of the dock. We still go there every year for our anniversary on my one day off.

As we were getting friendly with people there, we were talking at length about how we love seafood and the seaside, and the waiter told us about the Lobster Shack. We couldn't go there then, but the following year we went and fell in love with it so much. It takes you away from the festival just for a few hours.

We still go on my night off to Fishers Bistro – they have an extraordinarily huge range of seafood. But we make sure to go to the Lobster Shack at least a couple of times during the festival. Tony Law has gone down with his children too, as it's great if you've got children for the lido or the beach.

Tim Vine's been sent down, and Hardeep Kohli Singh—who is a food expert—had never heard of it. He said, I can't believe you've come all the way from Canada to introduce me to something Scottish.

Illustration by Gareth Morinan

197

DAVID WHITNEY
// ISLAND OF CRAMOND //

© Jesus Pizza

In 2010 I was in a film shot in Edinburgh called The Space Between, and a lot of it was shot on the island of Cramond, which is a beautiful and, dare I say it, magical place. If I need to get away from the madness I'll take a trip down there.

I also love running up Arthur's Seat and will be trying to start most my days that way. I also like stay up drinking till the early hours so my love of partying and my love of Arthur's Seat will be in constant conflict. The best case scenario would be to put a bar at the top

of Arthur's Seat.

"Cramond, which
is a beautiful and,
dare I say it, magical
place...."

Pub-wise I am very fond of the
Black Rose. It's a rock/Goth pub
so they all look miserable as a style
choice not just because their show
isn't selling well. The Jinglin Geordie
is also very close to my heart.

199

DRINK

DRINK

HOT BREW

DRINK

CASTLE

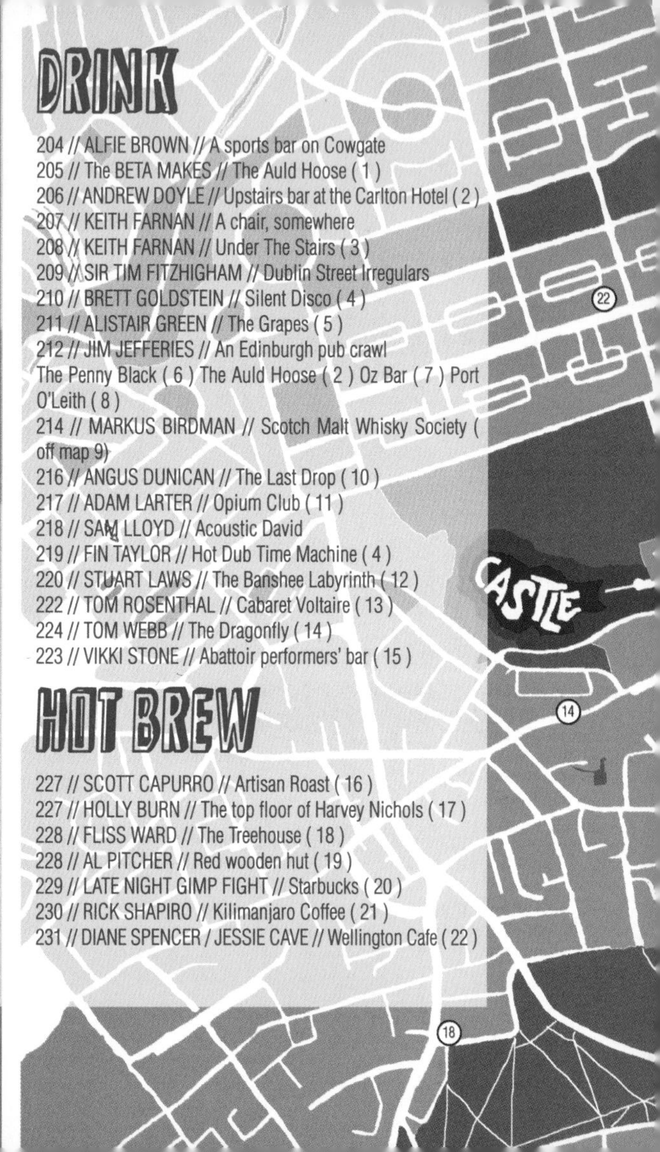

ALFIE BROWN
// A SPORTS BAR ON COWGATE //

Below street level, down damp, cobbled streets, beside rooms hiding ancient plagued bones lies a pub. A pub with multiple personality disorder.

> 'Am I a hotel?'
> 'No.'
> 'Am I a restaurant?'
> 'Certainly not.'

You might walk into this urine-sunk hellhole and manoeuvre yourself to the bar, overcoming the struggle of the intensely sticky floor. A gaggle of morons decorate the outskirts making loud noises as you try to negotiate your way around this maze, this pub, that looks as if it were designed by M. C. Escher when he was drunk. This is veering away from pub; this a dank booze multiplex.

However, there is a redeeming feature. If you manage to visit this place at the right time you might find that something wonderful is happening. Dripping walls are speckled with the glorious flat screen TVs that show sport. Men and women (men) gather to watch football, cricket and various forms of other completely pointless and yet completely fantastic SPORT.

Sy Thomas, James Redmond and I gather together each year with a new sense of hope, that perhaps anything could be possible, this year could be Liverpool's year. It hasn't been yet, but this year, this year could be the year; it won't be, but it could be.

No matter how awful the pub, it doesn't matter. In a month of meaning, vanity, reviews and pressure, a vacation is still a vacation even if it smells like sick. So come together Liverpool FC fans, Football fans and sports fans; let your brain have a little rest and let yourself convalesce by screaming at movement in different and pointless formations of colour and shapes. If you think sport doesn't matter I completely agree with you, but then, nothing matters, so could you shut up because Coutinho's through on goal?

THE BETA MALES

// THE AULD HOOSE //

The Auld Hoose, 23-25 St Leonards St, EH8 9QN. 0131 6682934, theauldhoose.co.uk.
Mon-Sat midday-00.45am, Sun 12.30pm-12.45am.

A solid month at the Fringe can feel like being locked in an abandoned warehouse and made to fight with the shambling figures of your own worst traits. Stay up all night! Drink a wheelbarrow full of bad booze! Eat things that have been fried at least three times! These ideas pummel you into submission until you resemble the Pillsbury dough boy after a six-month croissant bender.

Amidst this orgy of networking and panic and gin, it is important to find sanctuary. A safe space away from the noise and the nonsense. A place that offers peace, quiet and a jukebox full of aggressive metal. The Auld Hoose on St Leonard's Street has become a haven for the Betas over the years. A friendly goth pub (aren't they all?) with a rotating selection of real ales and a whisky menu to make a grown man weep.

For a little while, you're away from the Fringe and enjoying a pint of something hoppy while Vikings scream about pillage. We first stumbled through the doors of this tattooed Shangri-La as it was the nearest pub to our flat. Since then it has become a regular haunt. A place to celebrate, to commiserate, to order a plate of nachos so big that the teetering mound of delicious flesh and cheese stretches almost to the ceiling.

We love the Auld Hoose. For us it is as much a part of the Fringe as last-minute propcobbling and sixth-form drama groups lying motionless on the mile, flyers flinched between hopeful toes.

If this has inspired you to pay a visit to the Hoose, to have a nice glass of American Rye whisky as you attack a mountain of chilli, here's some friendly advice from the Betas: Don't. It's ours. Go away.

ANDREW DOYLE

// UPSTAIRS BAR, CARLTON HOTEL //

Carlton Hotel, North Bridge, EH1 1SD. 0131 472 3000, pumahotels.co.uk. Daily 11am-1am.

At the height of the festival, any attempt to traverse the full length of the Royal Mile is like an endurance test dreamt up by the Marquis de Sade. You end up having to negotiate dancers, minstrels, clowns, puppeteers, contortionists, poets, and occasional minor celebrities, all of whom are prepared to sacrifice their dignity for a few more ticket sales.

"The residents who drink there are a miserable lot. They look as though they only ever have sex to avoid conversation..."

After forcing my way through such a shameless display of collective desperation, I'm always left with a vague, uncomfortable feeling. Somewhere between psychopathy and sexual humiliation.

It is at moments like these that finding a quiet place to relax and have a drink becomes a priority. For me, I've always managed to find solace in the upstairs bar of the Carlton Hotel on North Bridge.

The residents who drink there are a miserable lot. They look as though they only ever have sex to avoid conversation. But it's spacious, it's quiet, and it's right in the centre of town. It simply doesn't occur to Fringegoers to drink here because it looks so posh and expensive. Actually, the price of drinks is no different from anywhere else.

So that's my tip for the Fringe if you are after some peace and quiet.

Of course, part of me hopes that nobody reads this. Otherwise I'll have ruined the whole thing.

KEITH FARNAN

// A CHAIR - SOMEWHERE //

It's a chair. It's as simple as that. I won't tell you where it is; suffice to say it is in a pub. But it's more than a chair. It's sanctuary. It's got a feeling of solidity and security that makes it feel like family, a family you actually like and get on with at Christmas.

With a high back surrounding you and perfectly-proportioned arms, it is a simple piece of furniture that wraps you up and coddles you from the ravages of a month of ups and downs not seen since the Rolling Stones mixed up their Xanax and their Quaaludes bags.

It is placed just next to a window facing another similar, but obviously not as perfect a chair so if you wish to entertain, you may, but if you wish to seek refuge from, well, everything in Edinburgh, you can just commandeer the corner.

Food seems more enjoyable, drinks seem bigger, colours seem brighter. Whether or not this chair has been laced with some sort of hallucinogenic fabric, I do not know. PCPolyester, Cocaineotton, Heroinylon, might all be present. It's rumoured to have inspired the song "Sit Down" by James.

It is the kind of chair Michael Caine could have sat in during the entire film of Zulu and felt untouchable. Marlon Brando would never have known "the horror, the horror" had he sat in this chair instead of on a throne of blood and bones. This chair makes Superman's Fortress of Solitude look like a Wetherspoon's on a Saturday.

I want to say there's a little bit of me in that chair, but that's probably unhygienic. It is vast. It is coveted. And there's probably some lucky bastard sitting in it right now. Damn him. Damn them all and their unappreciative hides.

KEITH FARNAN
// UNDER THE STAIRS //

Under The Stairs, 3A Merchant St, EH1 2QD. 0131 466 8550, underthestairs.org.
Mon-Sat noon-1am, Sun noon-midnight.

OK, so everyone else will have recommended Arthur's Seat and various museums and beautiful steps you stand on to see the dawn etc… and you're probably thinking, an Irish comedian will probably recommend a pub.

So I will not disappoint. When you're in the midst of the festival chaos for what seems like months, but is in fact only days, it is a joy to have somewhere relaxed, chilled and cool-without-being-pretentious to go to, and 'Under The Stairs' is my choice.

Besides the lovely Roald Dahl-inspiring name there's the location on the little hill between the Underbelly and the Gilded Balloon.

It's central to two of the biggest locations in the festival and yet you sneak in the back door of what I thought was the kitchen (which upset the manager when I asked where the main door was) and are greeted by soft armchairs, an array of fine foods, and a sense of peace that is rarely found in an Edinburgh pub but that slowly fades away into a pleasantly raucous evening…

So yes, Irish must-see is a pub…colour me stereotypical…

SIR TIM FITZHIGHAM
// DUBLIN STREET IRREGULARS //

My favourite place in Edinburgh is a tiny, not-very-well-advertised members' club on Dublin Street called the Dublin Street Irregulars. It is in a cellar which only seems to have two seats and a large rack of wine. The wine is free, which is better than the other clubs who seem to charge.

I believe the membership list was fixed at six people some time in the reign of the old Queen and has never expanded, which means there's always a very good chance of getting a seat: one in three (six members, two seats).

Directions to the Dublin Street Irregulars

wol at the Moon,

en follow the stars

TOP look d o w n

and where the stars meet the gutter

here you shall find the steps down to the

cellar

If not the Irregulars...the Ensign Ewart has always been a favourite for a pint or if the festival has got thoroughly too hectic then I love to head down to Leith.

Leith has so many happy mammaries, stunning fish restaurants and incredible pubs (Compass, Carriers, Port, Malt and Hops, Roseleaf to name a few).

A single by the shore after a hectic day at the festival is the greatest way to finish a day (that, and bugling in the sunrise from the top of Arthur's Seat, of course).

BRETT GOLDSTEIN
// SILENT DISCO //

I treat the Fringe like I treat a wedding: get on the dancefloor as fast as you can and stay on 'til closing. Make sure the music is loud. That way not only can you have fun dancing, but you can take a whole night off from talking to people without them knowing you hate them.

You just look like you're dancing. And there is no better place to do this than at the Silent Disco. (I appreciate this isn't exactly a secret in Edinburgh—I mean there are big signs for it everywhere—but you might have thought it was worth avoiding.)

Silent Disco is the best night out you can have in Edinburgh. Maybe You are given headphones with two channels that play you two different DJs. You can dance like an idiot and no one can judge you cos you can just pretend you're listening to the other DJ and that is why you have no rhythm.

And because you're wearing massive headphones, you can't talk to anyone. And best of all, if you take your headphones off, you can stand in a room, surrounded by these people we talked about, and for one blissful beautiful moment, they will all be, completely, wonderfully, silent. See you in there. Wave hello. I'll be the one listening to the other DJ.

ALISTAIR GREEN

// THE GRAPES //

The Grapes, 77 Clerk St, EH8 9JG. 0131 557 4522.

Edinburgh has much to offer in the way of pubs. There are many beautiful, traditional old boozers dotted around town where you can sit and have a pint in peace, away from the hustle and bustle of the Festival.

There are also the slightly rougher ones. The ones where eating a pickled egg makes you a pretentious snob, and the sound of an English accent is met with a look as if you had just walked in and announced yourself as the Duke of Cumberland. Those are the ones I like best.

The one I found last year will take some beating. One night I was in there and a young man was standing outside playing a flute. As I stepped outside to see what was going on, a drunk man in a stained suit walked past and deliberately knocked the flute out of the young mans mouth. Clearly rattled, the young man picked it back up and started playing again. Obviously not a woodwind fan, the drunk man then went for him again but the younger man was too quick and dodged out of his way.

Undeterred, the older man then bent down and dipped his finger in some dog poo that was on the kerb and pointed it at the younger man. He stopped playing his flute. The drunk man then turned towards the wall of the pub and slowly scrawled the word 'shit' on it using his stained finger, before staggering off down the street.

For a second everyone stood in silence. Clearly this was the best heckle any of us had ever witnessed. The younger man wandered off in the opposite direction, bewildered. I laughed like a little dog.

'You think that's funny?' a woman hissed at me, as if somehow this was all my fault.

JIM JEFFERIES

DRINK

I want to mention two of my favourite places in Edinburgh... both pubs, surprisingly.

Firstly, the Port O'Leith. I haven't been for a while but I used to disappear here when I didn't fancy having a mad night. I know it seems weird but when I'm around Bristo Square I normally end up still partying or drinking 'til gone 9am most mornings.

This pub has it all: great atmosphere, great people, the walls and ceiling has so much naval history and bits and bobs from all over the world hanging off it or stuck to it, and the drinks are reasonably priced, not £4 that most venues charge nowadays for a pint. So yes, check this place out!

Secondly my local—The Penny Black. I used to love sitting in there at about 7am with a Guinness and a whisky, watching people fall down the stairs and listening to the constant waffle around me and whoever I was with at the time.

Actually a few other pubs I like—why not? I should have done a top ten pubs to visit in Edinburgh during the festival.

The Auld Hoose at the top of the Pleasance. I remember it had the best jukebox in Edinburgh with AC/DC, Iron Maiden, Metallica and other great rock bands!

Last but not least is the Oz Bar on Candlemakers Row—I come here to watch the Aussie Rules, play pool and basically chill out before I have to go onstage.

It's really close to everything and always reminds me of home.

I'm bored of this and I've made myself thirsty, can I fuck off now?

THE PENNY BLACK
17 W Register St,
Edinburgh, City of
Edinburgh EH22
Tel: 0131 557 2879

PORT O'LEITH
58 Constitution St,
Edinburgh, Midlothian
EH6 6RS
Tel: 0131 554 3568

THE AULD HOOSE
23-25 St Leonard's St,
Edinburgh, EH8 9QN
Tel: 0131 668 2934

OZ BAR
33 Candlemaker Row,
Edinburgh, City of Edin-
burgh EH1 2QG
Tel: 0131 226 7190

MARKUS BIRDMAN

// SCOTCH MALT WHISKY SOCIETY //

The Scotch Malt Whisky Society, The Vaults, 87 Giles St, EH6 6BZ. 0131 554 3451, smws.co.uk. Mon-Wed 11.30am-11pm, Thu-Sat 11.30am-midnight, Sun 12.30-10pm.

During the month of August, you cannot move through the centre of Edinburgh without seeing posters, flyers, buses and taxis festooned with the hopeful mugs of a colleague. The city is awash with the technicoloured hopes and the dreams of the Creative. And every building is a venue, usually unsuitable. It's bloody everywhere.

One mile down the road, however, is Leith, where you'd be forgiven for not knowing that the festival is even on. And in August, as a comedian, that is a beautiful thing. It's a bit like being in a flotation tank, but wetter. It's an oasis of normality. An island of common sense. I love Leith.

But within that oasis, there's another oasis. Tucked up, between two Irvine Welshy-looking housing estates, in an 18th-century shipping vault on Giles Street, lies The Scotch Malt Whisky Society. It looks a hundred years old, but in fact was born in 1983 (a bit like someone who works for Avalon, in the last week of the festival).

What strikes you first is what a beautiful room it is. Leather sofas, oil paintings, reading lamps. It is a gentlemen's club, but everyone is

welcome. The next thing is the complete lack of pretension. Sure, if you know your whiskies, this is hog heaven. But you can know nothing and are not made to feel stupid by the enthusiastic, friendly and knowledgeable staff. You can say, 'well I had Bowmore once', and they won't say, 'who hasn't, you English twat'. Instead, they'll suggest you try Bowmore's 25 year old, where they only made 500 barrels.

Then they'll go, okay, so that's an Islay whisky, let's follow the coast road that distillery is on to another more boutique distillery, and try theirs. And then maybe go upstream inland to the next one and try their 30 year old that was made in 50 old sherry barrels imported from Jerez. Soon you'll be savoring unique whiskies, called Baby-faced Arsonist, Doctors' Surgeries and Flower Shops, and Gunpowder Treason and Plot.

You can even get decent food! In Scotland, unlike the whisky, this is not to be sniffed at. Then at the end of the evening when you're talking to an oil painting as if it's a dear friend, they'll even call you a cab home.

ANGUS DUNICAN

// THE LAST DROP //
The Last Drop, 74-78 Grassmarket, EH1 2JR. 0131 225 4851. Daily 10am-1am.

DRINK

The Grassmarket holds a special place in my heart as it is there one can find the Apex City Hotel, which played home to my one and only attempt to stage a play in Edinburgh: a whirlwind of precocious, pseudo-Beckett twaddle called Offensive Shadows (2004).

Opposite the hotel is The Last Drop. In that pub, someone told me that my play was 'utter genius'. They were catastrophically drunk but I helped them get more so by way of a thank you for their kindness.

In that pub I drowned my sorrows after my dressing room had been raided, taking my wallet which contained a Jedi braid. A braid that I had grown for four years and only cut off the day before. His name was Wilson.

In that pub, two years later, I sat with Pat Monahan (for whom my writing partner and I had been tasked with writing a sitcom vehicle) in complete silence for a whole evening because he was losing his voice. He communicated purely through hand gestures so it was a bit like hanging out with Harpo Marx but with more cuddling.

In that pub I told Aaron Barschak—the comedy terrorist—to fuck off 17 times in quick succession because he was trying to gate crash a domestic I was having with friend. The naked catharsis of it is something I cast my mind back to as a sort of meditative trance whenever I find myself confronted with the brash and tedious.

In that pub I drank alone last year, trying to start out writing my show for this year.

In that pub I will sit and have a drink on 11th August, 2013, and celebrate whatever happens on my Amused Moose final.

The Last Drop will always be the first place I drop into.

ADAM LARTER

// OPIUM CLUB //

Opium, 71 Cowgate, EH1 1JW. 0131 225 8382, opiumedinburgh.co.uk. Daily 8pm-3am.

It's important to note that as a teenage I lived in Weston-super-Mare and liked indie music.

There was no indie nightclub in Weston-super-Mare but there was a heavy metal nightclub, which would occasionally play Blur's Song 2 or Debaser by Pixies. For this reason I am very happy to be in a heavy metal nightclub and know all the words to Down With The Sickness.

Metalheads are the friendliest people ever and they have really interesting ways. Opium on Cowgate in Edinburgh is one of those amazing clubs and they do a great karaoke night.

In 2010 when starring in the hit show (some people liked it) The Very Best of Brice, Stephenson and Larter (with Ali Brice and Mark Stephenson) we had a BSL night-out and for some reason ended up at the karaoke night in Opium.

There were clearly no other festival-goers there that night and everyone was taking the karaoke VERY seriously. There were a lot of 'set pieces' with some very well rehearsed dancing. I did Song 2 by Blur (everyone agreed it was fantastic).

Mark Stephenson thought he could win a lot of friends by performing some Marvin Gaye. Mark waited for ages for the DJ to put him on and after a while it became clear that because of Mark's song choice it was unlikely he was going to get a go. The DJ called out for a guy called Hwang to come up on stage; Hwang wasn't about so Mark took that opportunity to say 'I'm Hwang' and have his song.

The best bit of that was that Mark had never heard the Doors' Touch Me, something very clear to everyone there that night. He performed the whole thing with one hand in his cardigan pocket. Amazing. Still my favourite night out in Edinburgh.

SAM LLOYD

// ACOUSTIC DAVE //

You can find out where Acoustic Dave is playing next on his Facebook page: on.fb.me/165gcQI.

Last year, while looking for a place to stumble out of at the end of the festival day, my wife and I wandered down the High Street and came across the sound of an acoustic guitar and a rockin' voice. This pub would become our favorite secret spot.

The singer was Acoustic Dave. He has the kind of voice that can deliver a Billy Joel ballad, and then belt out Back in Black by AC/DC the perfect example of a Not-Fair Voice. On this particular night he had the crowd literally bouncing around the place. A stocky woman at the bar had become so caught up in the excitement she decided bouncing on her stool was just not good enough. She bounced up onto the bar and began bouncing around up there.

She found a space between the beer taps and the cash register that her butt could just fit into comfortably and bounced away. However, as ideal as she felt the space was to a bouncing butt, it did have a drawback: one could only bounce forward or backward.

At the height of everyone's excitement, there was a violent thud when the woman's feet flew up in the air and she landed on her back on the other side of the bar. She had bounced backward. Rookie bar-bouncing mistake.

Everyone turned to see where the vibration had come from. My wife, having just moved to California, was under a table because I had recently shared with her some of my earthquake stories.

Acoustic Dave had the best view of the accident and stopped playing. The woman had survived and no permanent damage had been done, but everyone, including the woman, thought it best that she not be moved. So she bounced on her back behind the bar for the rest of the evening.

DRINK

FIN TAYLOR
// HOT DUB TIME MACHINE //

The Time Machine will be touching down at McEwan Hall throughout August. Visit hotdubtimemachine.com for specific dates.

Hot Dub Time Machine is simply the best night out on the Fringe.

It's a time-travelling disco taking you from Little Richard to Daft Punk via James Brown and Nirvana, which is always packed with sweaty, pissed comics trying to out-do each other in retro-dance-offs (as anyone who saw Joe Lycett, Romesh and I's three-way Running Man contest in 2012 will testify).

It used to be in a furnace of a room in the Gilded Balloon but rumours are it has moved to the McEwan Hall so it might be less sweaty but hopefully bigger and better. Then we can all go on to Palmyra. PARTAAAY.

// THE BANSHEE LABYRINTH //

The Banshee Labyrinth, 29-35 Niddry St, EH1 1LG. 0131 558 8209, thebansheelaby rinth.com. Mon-Thu 7pm-3am, Fri-Sun 5pm-3am.

© Banshee Labyrinth

It took me five years of gigging before I discovered where everyone was disappearing to during August; apparently Edinburgh is where aspiring comedians migrate to every year to flick a switch that turns them into superstars. 'Well colour me interested' I said and, in 2011, I performed at the Fringe for the first time. It was in a cellar in a pub called The Banshee Labyrinth and it was alright, although a bit like gigging anywhere, really.

19 performances, 20 minutes of new material and 21 better ways to finish this triumvirate later and I understood why comedians swam up the river. Performing stand-up is fun, enjoying it is why you start and you can forget that while slogging away in real life: Edinburgh reinvigorated me.

The Banshee Labyrinth was a new venue on the PBH Free Fringe that year and it has taken me two years to realise how lucky I was to have started there: it's one of the best small rooms in the city, including paid venues.

A highlight for me was, mid-performance, seeing what appeared to be a full-size yellow and black balloon dalek waddle past the room and dashing out to bring this interloper back into the gig for an unexpected finale.

That's what I think Edinburgh is about: seizing the unexpected and enjoying all that you can. Mainly because I couldn't find the superstar switch and no-one would tell me where it was.

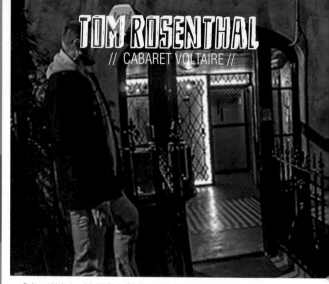

Cabaret Voltaire, 36-38 Blair St, EH1 1QR. 0131 247 4704, thecabaretvoltaire.com. Mon-Thu 4pm-3am. Fri-Sun midday-3am.

My favourite place in Edinburgh is the dingy yet delightful not-so-super club Cabaret Voltaire, complete with sticky Red Bull floors and stickier Red Bulled clientele. A complete release from the psychological and intellectual demands of an arts festival, Cabaret Voltaire offers an audience-free environment, where people are judged less for their stagecraft and more for a reluctance to put their hands up for Detroit.

Do try to scrum your way into one of the end of festival parties, thrown at someone else's half-lavish expense for some reason, and make your way to a dance floor populated by three categories of person:

» Comedians enjoying dance music far more than they should
» Comedians enjoying dance music far less than they should
» Agents trying to enjoy dance music the same amount as the comedians they represent.

My personal highlight of last year was seeing breakout American star Hannibal Burress, standing on the stairs betwixt the Magners-soaked bar and the sweat-soaked dance floor, with the Swedish House Mafia – via Edinburgh's finest speaker system – doing their best to knock him off his balance. As he looked towards the thronging jester's mire, the story across his face simply read: "I've done a Comedy Central Special. What the fuck is this?"

He never took a step closer, but remained, stoic—nay, afraid—on the stairs. I like to think that this year's breakout star will take the brave leap required, not letting a Scandinavian electro collective spook him or her quite so conclusively, to come and dance sweatily into the early hours with Naz Osmanoglu, Ivo Graham and Liam Williams.

Hopefully you'll be there to find out. You needn't do it at the 'end of festival Mick Perrin let's all drink for some reason shindig', you needn't do it alongside a premier up-and-coming comedian, but you need to spend at least one night breathing in the dirty delights of Cab Vol. It's open quite a bit. See you there.

TOM WEBB

// THE DRAGONFLY //

The Dragonfly, 52 West Port, EH1 2LD. 0131 228 4543, dragonflycocktailbar.com
Sun-Thu 4pm-midnight, Fri & Sat 4pm-1am.

Halfway along West Port, just tucked from sight of The Grassmarket is a cocktail bar. It can't speak, naturally, but if it could, it would tell you its name is 'The Dragonfly'. Luckily someone's written that on it

Decked out with seventies TVs, vinyl trays, porcelain tigers and fully-functional hand dryers, it is dead jazzy. They have also put a bar in it. I presume they have to. It's marble, if you're interested. With a little crook, two thirds of the way down.

That little crook is my favourite place in Edinburgh. Quite possibly, anywhere. I have had more fun and adventures and stories there than anywhere. None of which I care to share here—my mum might be reading this. (Hi Mum.) And whilst it's quite the commute from London, I do travel up there for a daiquiri whenever I can...

'Cause The Dragonfly is run by some of my best friends and is much cooler than I could ever hope to be, without ever coming close to making me feel that way, I genuinely adore it. It's also been home to three of my shows, including Tom Webb's Wedding... like I'm not gonna plug my show?!

If you ask nicely, or even if you don't, they will make you the best coffee, crispest beer, classiest cocktail or biggest laugh you could wish for. Particularly if you offer them a tequila. And if you wanna wind them up, ask for a mojito. But why would you do that?

It is like my very own Cheers, where, thanks to my show posters, everybody really does know my name. And if you would like to hear any of those aforementioned stories, I'll meet you at that little crook after my gig.

VIKKI STONE
// THE ABATTOIR PERFORMERS BAR //
Abattoir, Udderbelly place, Bistro Square, open late, good luck trying!

It's hard to narrow down my favourite place to escape from the Fringe, as the very nature of the Fringe means your escaping needs change depending on what you're currently sick of.

If it's for a late night drink away from the crowds, then it's the Udderbelly performer's bar Abattoir—it's like if The Groucho were made of cardboard, but with fewer rock stars and more chips.

If it is other performers I'm sick of, then it's a visit to the gym for a spot of light Zumba or a swim.

Love a bit of Zumba—particularly the way they don't teach you the moves, and everyone flails around trying to copy the dancing. It's like a group seizure to salsa music: the perfect antidote to constantly hanging around with talented people.

But this year I've got my puppy Bert with me, and I'm looking forward to hopping in the car one afternoon down to Berwick-Upon-Tweed for some quality beach dog walking.

He's never swam in the sea before, so here's hoping he likes cold water.

HOT BREW

SCOTT CAPURRO

// ARTISAN ROAST //

Artisan Roast, 57 Broughton St, EH1 3RJ. 07526 236615, artisanroast.co.uk. Mon-Thu 8am-7.30pm, Fri 8am-6.30pm, Sat 9am-6.30pm, Sun 10am-6.30pm.

A warm and cuddly POWERFUL coffee grinder and maker, this lovely little shop on Broughton Street has a library in the back, overlooking a garden. It's woodsy and calm, whilst the teaming trade that is the Edinburgh Fringe rushes by outside.

The java comes in many different tastes, from light to a darker, richer roast. The shop offers hot chocolate and tea I think, but who cares about tea?

Snacks are provided, but they're minimal. It's about the coffee, which is best drank alone, in the library, reading my pallid reviews. Pure, caffeinated joy.

HOLLY BURN

// TOP FLOOR HARVEY NICHOLS //

Harvey Nichols, 30-34 St Andrew Square, EH2 2AD. 0131 524 8388, harveynichols. com. Mon-Wed 10am-6pm, Thu 10am-8pm, Fri & Sat 10am-7pm, Sun 11am-6pm.

When I'm sick of the lot of you and fed up eating from miserable polystyrene cartons 'al fresco' in the freezing Courtyard, I take myself to Harvey Nicks top floor. I'll be honest: it's the only place I can find a decent Americano. I'm much more at home here. You can weep openly there, anonymously surrounded by the monied Morningsiders. I'll probably order a cheeseboard too.

DON'T COME AND FIND ME PLEASE – I'M TRYING TO GET AWAY FROM YOU ALL!

FELICITY WARD

// THE TREEHOUSE //

The Treehouse, 44 Leven St, EH3 9LJ. 0131 656 0513, facebook.com/treehouse.edinburgh. Mon-Sat 8am-5pm, Sun 9am-5pm.

As a whinging Australian, I wouldn't be perpetuating my stereotype if I wasn't complaining about food and the quality of UK coffee. So what a delight it was to shut me up when I was told about The Treehouse.

What a lovely little cafe this is. Excellent coffee. Great food. Right near the Meadows. And they serve breakfast late, which is an imperative during the Fringe, as it rarely happens before midday.

Spoon is also another great place to eat, and it is MASSIVE so you don't feel like people are sitting right on top of you.

AL PITCHER

// RED WOODEN HUT //

The hut we believe Al is talking about can be found at the top of Middle Meadow Walk

My little secret is a little wooden hut of food and coffee.

As you approach the Meadows from the Bristo Square end you will see this red wooden hut of destiny. Like most performers, I've had my ups and downs, and one morning five years ago I was down and nearly out at the Fringe.

I popped into this hut (only one and a half people fit in it, it's like Frodo's flat in the Shire) and I ordered a coffee and a bacon sandwich. But they had no frying pan, no oven, no grill. They cooked the BLOODY BACON sandwich under the steam of the

228

Upstairs in the Starbucks on the Royal Mile is just great for people watching. Grab an armchair by a window, sit back and wonder at the lengths brave young flyerers will go to as they delight and degrade themselves in equal measure for the attention of a few confused tourists. Musical theatre groups are particularly entertaining for this, for the obvious reasons. **LATE NIGHT GIMP FIGHT**

Starbucks, 124 High St, Royal Mile, EH1 1QS. 0131 225 4201, starbucks.com. Daily 6.30am-10pm.

...offee machine, it was incredible, it gave me hope.

...he Hut man was my MacGyver, he blew my mind. He let half of ...ne in and I cooked (steamed, warmed) some pig. It was the greatest ...ulinary delight ever.

...wonder if it's still there, or if it ever was there. Maybe it was part of ...show? If you do see it, go up to the hut and say what I was told, the ...rst rule of hut bacon sandwich cooked under a coffee machine club ...s you don't mention... oh.

RICK SHAPIRO

// KILIMANJARO COFFEE //

Kilimanjaro Coffee, 104 Nicolson St, EH8 9EJ. 0131 662 0135. Mon-Fri 7.30am-8pm.
Sat & Sun 8am-8pm.

In NY there are corner bodegas to get coffee at where you walk out of
your flat first thing in the morning, grab a coffee and a paper.

The guy behind the counter nods at you.

In Los Angeles, there are trendy coffee shops that are full of people
who think they are important because they wake up with attitudes,
reading magazines about tall thin people and drinking cappuccinos
that are half-decaffeinated wearing knit caps.

They wake up in their trendy knit caps with their chins in the
air—talking about mindless admissions of the awful screen play
they are writing, talking loudly on their phones about 'it's a great
day' and follow that by 'don't you just love it here', 'I don't live in
neighborhood, I live in a showcase for mannequins'...half-caf, de-caf,
single shot, room for milk, strong or weak...it's all bullshit, because I
just want a cup of coffee.

In Edinburgh I get my coffee at Kilimanjaro Coffee. Café Americano.
It's simple man; accept the simplicity, class and style of what I call my
neighborhood in Scotland. Most mornings you can find me there.

*See what Diane is talking
about at suchsmallportions.
com/dianespencer

DRINK

// WELLINGTON CAFE //

Wellington Coffee, 33A George St, EH2 2HN. 0131 225 6854. Mon-Fri 7am-6pm, Sat 8am-6pm, Sun 9am-6pm.

he beaten path? Like I have time in between flyering, doing the show, oing extra gigs, and making interviews/PR appearances to actually go nywhere. You know what, last year you guys asked me 'what madness ', and then seemed perturbed at the 5 minutes and 38 seconds answer I ave*. Stop asking such impossible questions, Such Small Portions.

ike anyone cares where Diane Spencer goes, 'which is off he beaten path'. I save my creative curious brain for living life, and xploring the world, which then translates into jokes, not finding some ackwater pub full of unwashed locals, or some pithy hillside spot where ou can watch a sunset, or THE MOST TRITE of all, a fucking café hat serves the best coffee in Edinburgh'...no, that place is Wellington Café, on George Street in the New Town.

hey send their baristas on coffee tasting/learning courses—I know, ecause I was living with one during the 2010 Fringe. Their scones are ivine. It's not a place you can necessarily get a table; it's really tiny, but if ou can hover by the bar, damn, they genuinely serve the best coffee in dinburgh. I have inadvertently answered your question. Fifteen all.

GET ACTIVE

TOM STADE

// GET CYCLING //

he room is dark, you have to know the password to get in, the music is pounding, you're wasted and its three in the morning.

here are hot, sweaty gorgeous women everywhere. And if your wife howed up you'd have a lot of explaining to do. Do you really want hat? 'Cause that's where most wide-eyed single comics with a false ense of what a good time is will send you.

Now listen to your uncle Tom. As a married guy who has lived in nd loved Edinburgh, I can't e seen in those compromising laces! We're not all single, ya now.

What people don't know is dinburgh has miles of awesome ike trails. Marriage-approved ctivity! You can't get more off he beaten path than that. What sed to be old rail lines are now ike trails.

> *"Edinburgh has miles of awesome bike trails. Marriage-approved activity! ..."*

t's healthy and relaxing, just riding. They wind in and out of the city.

o stop in Leith, walk for coffees or maybe you want to travel real eep and see some of Scotland's God-given beauty. See Edinburgh n your time. And when the one you loves asks you to explain ourself, you can rest easy and say: "I'm just trying find a place where we can be alone together so we can make out.

Let's get you all hot and sweaty."

HELEN ARNEY

// WARRENDER SWIM CENTRE //

Warrender Swim Centre, 55 Thirlestane Rd, EH9 1AP. 0131 447 0052, edinburghleisure.co.uk. Mon-Fri 7am-10pm, Sat & Sun 9am-6pm.

Swimming costume? Check.

Goggles? Check.

Towel? Check.

20p for the locker? Check.

Verruca sock? Maybe in the second week of August…

My Hidden Edinburgh is a jewel south of the Meadows, literally an oasis in the normality-deprived desert of the Fringe.

It is the Warrender Swim Centre. This is no Leith Waterworld, it remains regal and constant without flashy waterslides, wave machines and inflatable family fun times.

Hidden away on Thirlestane Road in Marchmont, the original 1887 bathhouse boasted a billiard room and a reading library. Today it has the modern equivalents (gym and yoga studio), but the original Victorian structure is still gloriously visible. It's like breaststroking back in time. It's like frontcrawling in an ancient cathedral. This is serious swimming for serious people.

Take the changing rooms. Lined up like beach huts on either side of the pool, you can walk straight out of your hut and into the water. There's no messing about about with footbaths, plastic overshoes and water wings here.

Then there's the lane etiquette. Three lanes are marked 'slow, medium and fast' (I've translated them as 'manageable, ambitious and insane') or you could dip into the other half of the pool, marked 'freestyle/dicking about'.

My preference is for the slow lane. You can't go any faster than the person in front, trying to overtake gives you no advantage and just tires you out, so instead just relax and enjoy the endless circular journey. A bit like the Fringe. It's my swimmer's take on Zen philosophy, and might help keep you sane well into week three.

Once you've overcome the lane anxiety, there are few things more relaxing than 40 lengths of backcrawl gazing through the expansive glass roof at the uniform grey of an Edinburgh summer sky.

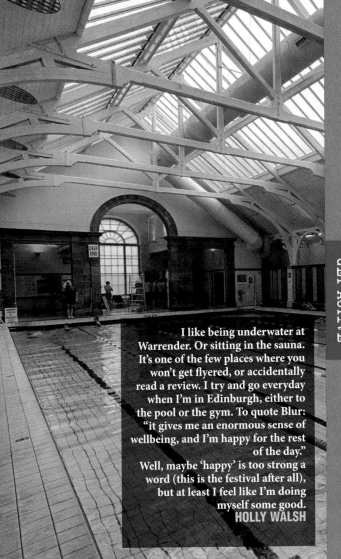

I like being underwater at Warrender. Or sitting in the sauna. It's one of the few places where you won't get flyered, or accidentally read a review. I try and go everyday when I'm in Edinburgh, either to the pool or the gym. To quote Blur: "it gives me an enormous sense of wellbeing, and I'm happy for the rest of the day." Well, maybe 'happy' is too strong a word (this is the festival after all), but at least I feel like I'm doing myself some good.

HOLLY WALSH

SARA PASCOE

// WARRENDER SAUNA //

My Favourite Place in Edinburgh is, um, is a sauna. On the side of Warrender Pool. I love it in there. It's all hot and dark, and womb-like (if I was a multi-birth).

I also enjoy being very close to strangers with not very many clothes on.

It makes me feel like a pack animal, just a few bald monkeys getting our sweat on. The main reason it's wonderful is because everyone there is a muggle and not doing an Edinburgh show, so you don't have to listen to them whining like you do all your real friends.

"I also enjoy being very close to strangers with not very many clothes on. It makes me feel like a pack animal..."

My favourite conversation was between two men in there last year. One (black pants) said "think the festivals started, there are posters" and the other man (blue speedos, hairier) replied "what – already?"

This was the 20th of August, the festival was almost over. "Are you going to see anything?" said blue pants.

"NO, I went one year, everyone kept going on about this show, 5 stars, 5 stars, 5 stars, and then I went…and it was just some guy with a microphone."

So that's good, isn't it? Whenever I'm getting all anxious about my career and my show and my self, I remember I'm just some guy with a microphone. Just some bald-monkey guy with amplification.

LUKE BENSON
// WARRENDER POOL //

It's a great leveller, the old Speedo. No-one's duds have stars on them, or quotes from the press, and they don't appear on the sold-out board. Plus there's no two-legged concoction of Am-Dram Smugma trying to stick a flyer in your goggles. It's perfect.

The pool also provides a little nostalgia-fest. It is a beautiful building, all mosaics and big windows. There's a picture of Mark Spitz talking to delighted Scottish kids while he's wearing just his wee kecks and one of the greatest moustaches of all time, telling them all about swimming, being healthy and winning medals. All things they'll never know anything about. Bless them.

It is also probably the only exercise you can do either hungover or still quite drunk with next to no risk of injury to oneself or others. If anything, mild inebriation helps to beat boredom when racking up the lengths, though I wouldn't recommend stashing a hip flask. Aqua-dynamics aside, the chafing is an atrocity.

HEFFERNAN & FLETCHER
// GLENOGLE SWIMMING POOL //

Glenogle Swim Centre, Glenogle Road, EH3 5JB. 0131 343 6376, edinburghleisure. co.uk. Mon-Fri 7am-10pm, Sat & Sun 8am-4pm.

As ladies of a delicate sensibility, when we've had up to here with the heckles, Heffernan and myself like to don our floral caps and stripey cozzies and head down to Glenogle Swimming Pool for a bit of old-fashioned back stroke.

We ease away the stresses of the festival and work off last night's gin at this Victorian oasis in Stockbridge. It has a lovely vaulted glass ceiling, a viewing balcony and one or two rather handsome lifeguards. I thoroughly recommend it.

ROSIE WILBY

// APEX POOL //

Apex Hotel, 31-35 Grassmarket, EH1 2HS. 0131 4410440, apexhotels.co.uk.

I've had quite an affinity with the swimming pool at the Apex Hotel on Grassmarket ever since I was one of the regulars on the synchronised swimming team at Liz Bentley's quite brilliantly bonkers Edinburgh on Sea (Edinburgh 2008). Every night an audience would sit around the edge dipping their feet in the pool and then often end up a part of the show by the end of proceedings. All of us women on the team sported rather fetching red polka dot bikinis from Primark.

One night guest performer John Hegley got into a dinghy to deliver a poem, wearing a very crisp smart shirt and trousers. Liz steadied it while he carefully stepped in – then it immediately capsized! Everyone gasped and then broke into fits of giggles as he surfaced and proceeded to deliver the poem quite calmly wandering around the pool with water dripping from his gesticulating arms. A genius moment! We never were really certain if he planned it all.

Other brilliant guests included Paul Foot, who regaled us with anecdotes as he swam up and down doing breast stroke.

We then used to peer up out at the midnight fireworks from the swimming pool windows and retire to the steam room for post show high jinx.

2008 was the year of persistent torrential rain so, even though we were performing in a swimming pool, we were no wetter than anyone else.

I returned to Apex on Grassmarket for my show the following year (though not the pool) and it has always been my favourite Edinburgh street, despite its rather gory history of being a site for public executions!

KARL SCHULTZ

// BANNATYNE HEALTH & FITNESS //

Bannatyne Health & Fitness, 43 Queen St, EH2 3NH. 0131 225 8384, bannatyne.co.uk.
Mon-Fri 6.30am-10.30pm, Sat & Sun 8am-8.30pm.

It's 2011, on the cusp of week two, with distemper rising. I was talking with myself along Cowgate one afternoon when who did we bump into but our good friend, choleric luvvie John Kearns. He appeared rouged with restored harmony. Apparently there was a secret gym way over the bridge with a pool and a jacuzzi and a sauna, all for £30 for the month.

While John and myself went to the Courtyard to look for fallen coins, straight to it I pruriently peregrinated out into the boondocks of the festival bubble to ferret out this aqueous Zion. Yeah, so turns out it was only a Bannatyne's gym...ah, but so naive! This was no health-off-the-shelf chain spa, but a sympathetic Shangri-La rubber-stamped by Entertainers of a certain age – pure anecdotal manna for we Brookes-sight courtiers! Actually, I don't know that that is what it was at all, having only attended on the day I signed up. But what a day! Indeed just as I was tergiversating my turpitude on the dotted line who do I see beside me, rouged in a rented bathrobe, but the mahatma of the Assembly Mound himself Simon Callow! "How's the play, Simon?" "WONDERFUL BOYYY!"

Half an hour later I was on the third floor and did lightning strike twice! Fame Academy's Ruby Wax happening just ten feet away, rouged in tenacious lycra (presumably not rented). While I slowly geared into some passionless hammer curls, in chance propinquity, she arched backwards over a silver Swiss ball and held barbing eye contact with me for what may've only been an inexpedient turn, but distended into an epoch. All to the dolent entreaties of 'Papa Can You Hear Me?'

I tell you, you may go there and hear Simon slamming on the reception bell crying "THERE'S SOMETHING IN THE JACUZZI!" or you may just moderately improve your cardio. Either way it brought me so many Likes Apunda started speaking to us again. Gluckliche Reise!

ANGELA BARNES

// SCOTSMAN HOTEL SWIMMING POOL //

Scotsman Spa, 1 Market St, EH1 1TR. 0131 622 3800, scotsmanspa.com. Mon-Fri 6.30am-10pm, Sat & Sun 8am-8pm.

Last year, on arriving in Edinburgh, I was full of great intentions of exercising and writing every day between the two shows I was doing. Ha!

On recommendation of my friend James Redmond, I joined the Scotsman gym as it had a pool. My relationship with the Scotsman got off to an inauspicious start. I rocked up slightly bedraggled (got caught in a downpour, in Edinburgh. I know!) to join up for the month. A snooty receptionist looked me up and down and said "you do know that's £75 don't you?". I said 'yes' and paid up. He didn't even show me around, so I left feeling embarrassed and angry. James hadn't been treated like that when he signed up. But he is pretty and used to be in Hollyoaks, so...

I complained to the management and got a full apology, an induction and was given a free massage. Despite this, the pool at the gym became my absolute sanctuary in Edinburgh 2012. I think I may have become a cold-hearted killer had it not. And that receptionist would have been target numero uno.

I used the gym just once. During that first workout I turned around, sweating and looking like Lee Evans after a particularly vigorous arena show, to see the perfectly coiffured partnership of Tom Deacon and Chris Ramsey sat astride adjacent weights machines with nery a sweat molecule between them or a hair out of place. And I decided at that point to stick to the pool.

The pool is a dimly lit, warm haven with 'sun' loungers where, if you squint, you could be on the Med. I happily spent most afternoons alternating between swimming, saunaing, steam rooming and staring at a blank notebook. And the best thing about the pool at The Scotsman? There is not a poster or a flyer in sight. Bliss.

LUCY PORTER

// BRISTO YOGA SCHOOL //

Ashtanga Yoga Edinburgh, 43 Argyle Place, EH9 1JT, 0131 228 7581, ashtangayogaedinburgh.com. Mon-Fri 10am-8pm, Sat 9am-2pm, Sun 3-7pm. Longer hours during the festival.

When I was up at the festival in 2010, I wasn't doing a show, I was heavily pregnant, and just up there to support my husband who was performing. I had intended to go and see loads of shows, but I hadn't taken into account the baking hot venues, cripplingly uncomfortable seats, and the fact that a baby pressing on my bladder would make it impossible to sit still for an hour.

I wanted to find ways to relax and luckily I discovered Bristo Yoga School. It was tucked away right in the middle of the festival on Bristo Place, and was a welcome contrast to the shouting, hustling, flyering bustle outside. Last time, obviously, I went to the pregnancy yoga classes, but I'll be going back this year to 'normal' ones at their new site at Ashtanga Yoga if I can, to bend, stretch and unwind from the festival madness.

I'm also intending to head to the floatarium in Stockbridge to immerse myself in the sensory deprivation tanks. I should be the most chilled-out comic at the fringe. The only way I could have a more hippy festival would be if I was doing a show called 'Lucy Porter – Dreamcatcher' in a hand-knitted yurt.

DAVID QUIRK

// TRANSGRESSION SKATE PARK //

Transgression Park, 10B Kings Haugh, EH15 5UY. 0131 661 4769, transgressionpark.
com. Mon-Fri noon-10pm, Sat & Sun 10am-2pm.

I'm glad I do comedy for many reasons, but one is to help curb my vast intake for riding a skateboard.

I would surely do it every day if I wasn't concentrating on shows and such. I haven't been to Edinburgh since 2010, and then I was so busy doing two shows a day that I only visited the Edinburgh skate park once, on my one Monday off.

I got on a girl's bike that I'd borrowed from the English students I was staying with and rode for a little under an hour to the skate park. It was fun and I met some cool kids. They were literally kids. I'm 32. Oh well.

Coming from Melbourne, Australia, skate parks are in abundance and I'm spoilt. Edinburgh less so, until five minutes ago, however there is one place called Transgression Skate Park; it's new, it's indoors, and it's in town!

I'm not sure about the name of it but it does strangely have something in common with the themes in my show. My show is transgression heavy! This new place will be my salvation when I'm not performing, flyering, drinking or sleeping. Here's to not breaking anything!

LOVED & LOST

While compiling this guide some of the places we were recommended by comedians have unfortunately moved on, however we felt that we'd give you a taster of what they were anyway.

JOANNA NEARY

Finding the Royal Antediluvian Order of Buffaloes Social Club coincided beautifully with being too old to stop up all night for a whole month anymore. Going there was like collecting a cuddle from life outside the Fringe.

I love this venue so much but it's not for everyone. My friend who met me there and is used to the camaraderie and ostentatiousness of certain other Fringe festival venues sat in tolerant silence, clearly hating it and left as quickly as possible. At that moment I decided we had grown apart.

This little social club is a small paradise in Edinburgh if you like the following things:

- An anti-atmosphere. Also known as…

- An oasis of calm, tranquillity and normality with Edinburgh locals and a small number of performers, sitting side by side in perfect harmony, united by their preference of being able to converse quietly and unassumingly with really cheap booze, seemingly away from any hint of being at a massive festival, even though it's actually a venue itself. I don't know how they did that.

- Rooms, which could feasibly hold memorably good, jumble sales.

- Crisps in The Three Main Flavours.

- Chocolate for sale.

- Very friendly staff, proud to be selling cheap, good booze and welcome snacks.

- Walls covered in oil paintings of monarchs and lords hung at jaunty angles.

- Functional seating and loads of room.

Pretending (to yourself only, not loudly or in theatrical mime – try the Udderbelly for star jumping displays) that you're on the set of the bar in Saturday Night, Sunday Morning.

That weird wall covering that seems to be plywood with holes drilled at regular intervals and stops you feeling posh.

Reasonably priced Appetiser.
And it's open to late an all.
DISCLAIMER: THIS IS MY MEMORY OF A VENUE I FIRST WENT TO ONE EDINBURGH FRINGE (2011) WHEN GOING TO SEE ROBIN INCE'S BRILLIANT PBH FREE FRINGE SHOW AND FACTS MAY BE FOGGED BY TIME AND AGE. WHY NOT HAVE AN EXCITING ADVENTURE AND LOOK FOR IT YOURSELF? YOU'RE WELCOME!)

ANDREW O NEILL
// ALTERNATIVE CLOTHES STORES //

All of my favourite places in Edinburgh seem to disappear. There was Flip - one of those alternative clothing shops that every city in Britain has, where I'd buy at least one t-shirt every year until it closed.

That honour has now shifted to Electric Cabaret, the goth / alternative shop on Forrest Road. They sell the wonderful vegan Iron Fist shoes, lots of black clothes with buckles and straps and bells and whistles on, to suit the 14 year old goth in your family.

They also have a brilliant range of t-shirts and stripy things and some great corsets. And the proprietor dresses like a pirate 24/7. He is a complete dude. Next door is the Creepy Wee Shop In The Graveyard, in Greyfriars Graveyard. They sell a wicked collection of skellington-based tat, although it seems to be closed more often that it's open.

Jordan Valley on Nicholson Street sells wonderful vegan food and the guy who runs it will usually get you to try some spicy paste he's made which will be delicious. I think he might be a wizard, too.

CHRIS COX
// CHOCOLATE SOUP //

If I'm meeting someone for a cuppa and need a bit of a sugar fix I will always get them to meet me at Chocolate Soup.

It's well handy being right off the Royal Mile and does the sickliest, but most delightful hot chocolates you could want. It's always far too busy and full of people yet I seem to be able to nail getting a table and stuffing my face with chocolate.

You'll tell if I've been in there. I will have chocolate round my mouth and staining at least one piece of my clothing.

LEWIS SCHAFFER
// GOOD 2 GO //

My favorite place in Edinburgh is the Good-2-Go cafe at 37 West Nicolson Street across from The Counting House and The Pear Tree I sit in the corner of the shop (and it is so tiny it only has a corner) and safely watch the chaos of the festival marching down West Nicolson Street, streaming in and out of the Counting House.

I see the Counting House kitchen window, where I put a fan to extract the hot air from the Ballroom, the simplest of solutions (and the most effective) to Edinburgh's chronic venue heat problem, and was met by fierce resistance.

It was my insistence on the fan that got me banned. Now experience my show at The Hive on Niddry Street!
I love the Polish owner Paulina Rachowska.

When I first met her I saw her as concentration camp guard – all snarling and mean. Now I know she is a righteous protector of the weak – I am weak - yes me! I think if you mention my name, she might snarl at you, too, and then treat you very, very nicely.

MISCELLANEOUS

Fun, entertaining and amusing as they are, the following contributions simply don't fit into any category

TERRY CLEMENT
// HIS 28TH APPEARANCE //

Terry Clement has never performed at the Edinburgh Fringe Festival, nor has he ever been to Edinburgh. Despite it all, Clement insists that this is his 28th appearance.

"I took ten years off to investigate the merits of certain substances. Otherwise, this would actually be my 38th Fringe show." Mr Clement reports while rolling something into a 'blunt' wrap.

We asked him about the funniest thing that happened to him over the years at the Fringe. Through bales of smoke he paused then said, "One night I was doing an impression of myself and that's the one show that I also just happened to be in the audience. I stood up in the crowd and yelled something like, "I'm not like that!" to me on stage...strangest heckle I've ever given or received."

HARRY DEANSWAY
// COMEDY 1 : EDINBURGH 0 //

The Edinburgh Fringe: one of the world's great secrets, with its million-plus visitors every year. But what is my Edinburgh secret? My deep fried Mars bar, wrapped in a mystery, inside a haggis, if you will.

Well, it's the only shop in Edinburgh where you can find vegetables that aren't left over from medieval times...haha brilliant! I jest of course, this is a light-hearted piece after all and I am a 'comedian'. We all know there are no vegetables in Scotland let alone any from medieval times. BOOM! Comedy 1 Edinburgh 0

My Edinburgh secret is my dislike of The Fringe. There is better weather on the moon in the month of August; the 16 hours you are not either performing or sleeping you are having to feign interest in how some poor fellow act's show is going; and you can't even afford a drink to drown your sorrows as you have spent all your money on what at the same cost in any other country would be palatial accommodation but in Scotland is one step up from a tent.

I am sorry if I have drawn the wizard's curtain too far back, but this my friends is the reality and hopefully like my career after you've read this is now no longer a secret.

LEE KERN
// HIS OWN SHOW //

The Edinburgh Comedy Festival is a wonderful idea. Take the most neurotic, bitter and jealous people in society – comedians – then put them all in the same town for a month. Then – as an added bit of fun – just to mix things up a bit more – put them into competition with each other. Stand back and watch the good times roll. For a whole month Edinburgh becomes a crackling pleasure dome of angsty nervous energy.

Where is a wonderful, secret place during the Edinburgh festival? I guess any place where there are no comedians talking about their show. So that's any pubs, shops, streets or public spaces out of the equation. Libraries, zoos, restaurants, food stalls - they're no good. The sewers are out cos that's where the critics go. You can't go to your flat cos you live with other comedians. There is not a single square inch of Edinburgh that hasn't been colonised by clowns for this month. So where is a secret place? Where is some virgin ground that nofootprint of oversized clown's shoe has trodden? Where can one go to escape all this laughter? Come to my show, Lee Kern: Bitter Twitter, every day at the Gilded Balloon at 8.15pm. That'll do as a start…

NB: The above payoff is not true – my show is incredibly funny and I'm funny and friendly like a classic feelgood entertainer (eg. The Krankies or Chris De Burgh).

MCNEIL & PAMPHILON
// THEIR FLAT //

Our Secret Edinburgh place is our flat. We snagged a lovely place a little bit out of town last year that is the opposite of the horror stories you hear about people's accommodation – it's great to have somewhere Away from the chaos to retreat to.

Whilst it is quite rare for comedians at the Fringe to see their flat whilst sober, being the tender age of 32, there is nothing we like more than heading home for an early night, getting into our matching pyjamas (no, really, Sam forgets his every year and ends up wearing Steve's spare pair) and watching some excellent telly. Last year Sam watched 'The London Riots' on 'The News' which Sam felt was 'edgy, well acted, but ultimately not very realistic.' Steve preferred the flat's wide selection of Disney DVD's (again, true), which makes him a little bit like Thom Tuck, though Steve failed to write a single joke about it.

This year we'll be sharing the flat with the wonderful Garrett Millerick and Dave McNeill, who both have great shows at the festival. The house is sure to be full of mirth or, more likely, pizza boxes, cheap lager and farts.

GEORGE RYEGOLD
// STALKING //

The urge to escape Edinburgh during the Festival Fringe seems a preoccupation for some. So what better than an escape that offers all the fun of both solitude and voyeurism? Nothing. Nothing better.

Whenever the enthusiasm, hope and boundless joy of everybody except myself thrusts its pointed, jubilant spear into the black entrails where my soul squats, I need merely to back myself into one of the splendidly dark nooks, gouged from the walls of the Royal Mile, holing myself up in Roxburgh Close like a Trapdoor spider, and bserve the mortal goings-on of the thoroughfare unheeded.

There are many of these sultry havens running directly off the Mile
– the tantalizingly-monikered Fleshmarket and the, sadly renamed,
Lyon's Close which used to be more truthfully known as 'Stalker's
Close'.

The silhouette of one's lurking bulk at the end of the passage is often
enough to keep it to oneself. Should anyone intrude upon your
solitude in the event of a light shower, a sinister silence in response
to their salutations and a snarl at the tepid, cheesy tang of their damp
outdoor-wear is often enough to keep their stay to a minimum.

If one were more flexible, one could kick oneself in one's balls."

ACKNOWLEDGEMENTS

First and foremost, we thank all the acts from the bottom of our hearts. How many other industries can you put out a call for a book like this and get over 150 acts deliver the goods within a few weeks?

With our website we have always aimed to be positive about - and to support - the boundless creativity of people who work in comedy and this project has helped confirm our faith in that. We promise to continue doing what we can to help connect comedians with audiences. Make sure you support them too...

There's a whole host of people who went above and beyond the call of duty to help us get the acts on the page. Particular thanks are due to Michael Loveless for the brilliant cove design; Nica Burns for embracing our little project so readily; Alex Brenner for allowing us to use his images for the book (particularly Mark Thomas), the unstoppable Bex Colwell; the ever-professional Paul Sullivan, David Burns and Sally Carter; the endless patience of Ben at Multitude, Brett Vincent for offering up his acts so readily, Christy at Emery PR and Amée at Prospero; the endless exclamation marks of Flick Morris and Gaby at Neil Reading PR; the indefatigable Beth at Ditto and Susanna at RBM; the eye for detail from Lee at Gag Reflex and Chris at Phil McIntyre Ents; and the superb teams at PBJ, Lisa Thomas Management and DAA Management; The Comedy Ad Network guys: Mark Boosey, Paul Fleckney and Andrew Dipper for their own help and support over the years; Ed Vass, Matt Lacey and Perri Lewis for their help navigating the world of book publishing; Mustafa at Mega Print for his patience with an ever-expanding print deadline. Tamara Cowan for her hard work, and last of all Gemma Griffiths - without whom this simply would not and could not have happened at all.

Edited and produced by Tim Clark and Andrew Mickel
Production and design by Tim Clark
Maps drawn by Tim Clark
Subbing and proofing by Gemma Griffiths
Cover art by Michael Loveless from Tk Tk To :
facebook.com/ticktacktoedesign

ABOUT SUCH SMALL PORTIONS

Such Small Portions is a website all about comedy. We've been plugging away since 2007, covering The Laughs from Vancouver, Austria and New Zealand. To be honest, though, we're normally just in the United Kingdom.

Run by journalists Tim Clark and Andrew Mickel, we do news and features, with prolific interviews, live comedy recommendations and much more. We also do live events, from a comedy cook-off competition at the Leicester Comedy Festival to decorating a shed with pictures of comedians at Latitude.

Why read us? Well, for a sector based on being funny, we're perpetually amazed at how serious everyone is. Sometimes all you want to do is make comedians get into fights over puddings, poke a drunk Doug Stanhope with a metaphorical stick, or get Emma Kennedy to get into a long-winded anecdote about the sex drive of dwarves.

(That got us on to page nine of Google for 'dwarf sex'. We're working on getting higher.)

WHAT'S WITH THE NAME?

Such Small Portions is based on the opening sketch of Woody Allen's Annie Hall, about two old ladies in a cafe in the Catskill Mountains. The food is awful, they say, but even though they can't stand it, they still can't get enough of it.

With this joke Allen manages to sum up one of life's great ironies: that though we may complain and moan throughout the duration of our lives, the whole thing is over all too quickly. With that mantra firmly placed within our heads, the main ethos of SSP is to delve into comedy as well as report on it, getting our hands dirty and turning up in unexpected places. Like Leicester.

CONTRIBUTOR INDEX

PLACE INDEX

ABOUT THE AUTHORS

TIM CLARK   04/07/2013

ANDREW MICKEL   04/07/2013

Tim Clark is a freelance travel and entertainment journalist based in London, UK.

Tim helped found the Such Small Portions site as a student in 2007 and has a keen interest in both travel writing and comedy, somehow managing to link the two more often than should be allowed. Favourite comedy endeavours include helping to organise a comedy cook off, decorate a garden shed at Latitude with comedy fan art, reporting from Altitude Festival in France and Austria and delving into the wilds of Canada on the Snowed In Comedy Tour.

Despite his love of travel he's absolutely useless at foreign languages.

Andrew Mickel is a London-based journalist who splits his time between comedy and entertainment and health and social care. (Doctor Phil Hammond is the only person who has helped him transcend said boundary.)

He has interviewed a rather hefty percentage of comedians currently on the circuit and has a soft spot for light-hearted acts you want to gossip with (Joe Lycett) and deep and meaningful acts you want to have a heart to heart with (Doctor Brown).

He never quite got over Pulling getting axed.

They have won Baftas, comedy awards, critical acclaim and are among the best-known faces in the business, but can a group of comedians compile a travel guide to the city they hold close to their hearts?

Secret Edinburgh is the combination of the musings, fables, exploits and raucous night-time antics of over 170 comedy acts who penned their own secret recommendations to the Scottish capital.

With contributions from Marcus Brigstocke, Mark Thomas, Milton Jones, Isy Suttie, Susan Calman, Shazia Mirza, Jim Jefferies, Josh Widdicombe, Joel Dommett, Tony Law, Joe Lycett, Zoe Lyons, Eric Lampaert, Phil Nichol, Sara Pascoe, Jay Foreman, Holly Walsh, Richard Vranch and many, many more...

UK £7.99
© Such Small Portions
Cover art by Michael Loveless
HUMOUR / TRAVEL
www.suchsmallportions.com

ISBN 978-0-9926209-0-5

9 780992 620905